BEFORE & AFTER

Biblical Principles for a Successful Marriage

By Carl E. Taylor & Charity Taylor

Harrison House

Tulsa

DEDICATION

We would like to dedicate this book in memory of Bishop Harry S. Thompson and Rev. Jean P. Thompson, Charity's parents and our pastors for over 20 years at Lighthouse Tabernacle Ministries in Staten Island, NY. They gave us a great foundation in the Word of God and built within us the importance of maintaining a personal relationship with the Lord Jesus Christ. They were our spiritual parents, mentors, and friends.

We would also like to dedicate this book to the memory of our former pastor, Billy Joe Daugherty, and to our current pastor, Sharon Daugherty at Victory Christian Center in Tulsa, OK. They demonstrated a living example of many of the principles discussed in this book. Their love for God, family, and all people brought us to another level of understanding how to walk in God's unconditional love.

Special thanks to Pastor Sharon Daugherty, Dr. Cal Easterling, PhD, Katie and Gregg Armour, Daniel and Kelli Mackey and Joel and Ester Matu for their help in editing and sharing their comments and/or testimonies for this book. We love and appreciate all of you and count it a blessing and a privilege to know you.

We also want to recognize the Victory Sunday School administrative staff who asked us to teach the *Before You Say I Do* class at Victory Christian Center (VCC). We believe they were truly led by the Spirit of God and helped us to find our place in VCC.

We would also like to dedicate this book to all the couples and friends who we met while teaching this class.

PREFACE

For those not yet married, the purpose of this book by Rev. Carl and Charity Taylor, my precious friends and co-laborers in the Lord's vineyard, is two-fold:

1. To prevent a terrible marriage. If we know why marriages go wrong, we are better able to set new marriages on a proper pathway to blissful adventures of togetherness. Many young people confound their elders with this paradox— they ponder long and hard over the choice of a career, but marry on what seems like the spur of the moment. They will take career analysis tests and consult family and friends for their judgment on the proper choice of a job, but disregard a similar process of due diligence in the establishment of a supposedly lifelong relationship.

2. To help initiate a marriage that is a howling success—a wonderful and happy marriage. If you want to get to the fiftieth wedding anniversary with a joyous and ecstatic loving relationship with your spouse, read this book!

For those who are already married, this fine book will enhance your relationship and help you recover from any presumably "irreconcilable" differences. At the very least, it will remind you of principles for marital happiness that you may have forgotten in the process of overcoming the many struggles of day-to-day living.

Marriage is a covenant—a binding reciprocal agreement **of the parties** *to take each other, not for granted, but for wedded wife and wedded husband until parted by death. In the wedding ceremony, they join their hands together and exchange rings. Wedding rings are today's sub-*

stitute for the old practice of cutting the thumbs and placing dirt or gunpowder in the wounds as a permanent sign of the marriage covenant. A clergyperson pronounces that they are man and wife.

Is a wedding necessary? Isn't it just an old-fashioned tradition of saying a few words and then going about life as you were before except that you are now together with a spouse? *Au contraire*, living together outside of marriage is sin. It is not some "small" sin you can just ignore, either. It is fornication and no fornicator shall see the Kingdom of God.

> *I Corinthians 6:9 Know ye not that the unrighteous shall not inherit the kingdom of God? Be not deceived: neither fornicators, nor idolaters, nor adulterers, nor effeminate, nor abusers of themselves with mankind, 6:10 Nor thieves, nor covetous, nor drunkards, nor revilers, nor extortioners, shall inherit the kingdom of God*

> *Galatians 5:19 Now the works of the flesh are manifest, which are these; Adultery, fornication, uncleanness, lasciviousness, 5:20 Idolatry, witchcraft, hatred, variance, emulations, wrath, strife, seditions, heresies, 5:21 Envyings, murders, drunkenness, revellings, and such like: of the which I tell you before, as I have also told you in time past, that they which do such things shall not inherit the kingdom of God.*

> *Ephesians 5:5 For this ye know, that no whoremonger, nor unclean person, nor covetous man, who is an idolater, hath any inheritance in the kingdom of Christ and of God. 5:6 Let no man deceive you with vain words: for because of these things cometh the wrath of God upon the children of disobedience.*

Marriage is the plan of God, as He demonstrated with Adam and Eve and by the presence of Jesus at the wedding in Cana of Galilee, where He performed his first public miracle. The family is God's chosen means of organizing societies. The family is the most important agent of socialization in a child's life and determines—to a tremendous extent—what kind of person that child will be.

Pay heed to the words of wisdom in this book. It is based upon the bedrock of the Word of God and birthed in the Spirit of God. It is informed by the many years of teaching and gentle guidance Carl and Charity have so freely given in the Sunday School ministry of Victory Christian Center. They have been invited to and attended more weddings than most of us could imagine, because their students so appreciate the wisdom and understanding gained through this method of instilling God's principles for righteous, moral, and happy living within the stable boundaries of a Godly marriage.

Have a happy day!

Cal Easterling, Ph.D.

Sunday School Superintendent

Victory Christian Center

Tulsa, Oklahoma

TABLE OF CONTENTS

FOREWORD

Carl and Charity have been married for 28 years, and over the past five years they have been ministering to couples, teaching principles for having a healthy marriage relationship.

This book provides practical guidelines that will help couples identify their strengths and weaknesses in order to close the door in any vulnerable areas that would potentially divide them. They provide scriptural counsel on how to better relate to one another and grow stronger through the tests of time.

I am grateful for the many marriages they have helped to save because of their ministry. This book helps couples understand how to walk out their love for one another.

Sharon Daugherty

Senior Pastor

Victory Christian Center, Tulsa, OK

INTRODUCTION

"He who finds a wife finds a good thing, and obtains favor from the LORD."[1]

On May 4, 1985, Charity and I were married. We were young and in love, but didn't really know what love meant. Had we known what lay ahead of us, we would have taken more time to prepare ourselves for the challenges we would face. As with many Christian couples who have been married for 25 years or more, we look back and realize it was God's love for us and our love for Him that kept us together all these years.

Many people believe that you just fall in love, however we like to say that we've grown in love through the love of God in us. This love grew and developed through the many tests and trials that we faced along the way. Love that does not stand the tests of life is not true love. According to I Corinthians the 13th chapter, love never fails. This is the foundation on which to build your marriage.

The Lord put the desire in our heart to write this book because of the high rate of divorce in Christian marriages today. From the Garden of Eden until now, God has not changed His desire for us to have and enjoy a fruitful marriage filled with an everlasting love. However, it is not a storybook marriage where nothing ever goes wrong, nor is it a marriage that never experiences challenges. It is a marriage that will grow stronger through every adversity. Romans 8:35-39 states that nothing can separate us from the love of God. God expects us to use that same love to love one another unconditionally. The degree to which you will love your spouse is determined by the degree that you love God and have experienced His love in your own life. You cannot give what you

---

[1]Proverbs 18:22 NKJV

do not have, and if you do not have a revelation of the God kind of love, you will not be able to give that kind of love to your spouse.

God's Word says, *"My people are destroyed for lack of knowledge: because thou hast rejected knowledge, I will also reject thee, that thou shalt be no priest to me: seeing thou hast forgotten the law of thy God, I will also forget thy children."*[2] We can see that this has come true today, even in the lives of Christians who have forgotten what the Word of God has to say about marriage.

It is our intention that this book be used as a resource, not just in times of crisis, but as a tool to maintain the spiritual unity and oneness in marriage that Jesus spoke of in Matthew 19:5-6 when He said, *"For this reason a man shall leave his father and mother and shall be united firmly (joined inseparably) to his wife, and the two shall become one flesh? So they are no longer two, but one flesh. What therefore God has joined together, let not man put asunder (separate)."*[3]

In a world that is trying to redefine marriage, we desire to see the love of God prevail through the example of Christian marriages that are founded on the Word of God. We are called to minister the love of God to couples and in doing so, help eliminate a lot of unnecessary divorces in the Body of Christ. Romans 12:2 says that we should not to be conformed to this world, but be transformed by the renewing of our minds. That's exactly what it's going to take to see God's love prevail in marriages today. This may seem like an impossible task, but God never gives us something that we can do without Him.

God has helped Charity and me turn our differences into opportunities for personal growth and maturity. For instance, Charity likes apples; I like oranges—so we make a smoothie!

---

[2] Hosea 4:6 KJV
[3] Matthew 19:5-6 AMP

CHAPTER 1

WHOLENESS

DISCOVERING THE HOLES

Before entering into a serious relationship with the intent of marriage, it is important to take the time to examine your life to see if there are wounds that need healing. These often painful experiences are potential pitfalls, or holes, that could cause problems in the development of a successful marital relationship. *A **hole** is an opening, a hollow place, an embarrassing position or predicament, a fault or flaw.*[4] Holes can be caused by many things such as:

- the loss of a loved one

- divorce

- the breakup of a long term relationship

- child abuse

- sexual abuse

- dealing with your own or someone else's addiction to drugs, alcohol, etc.

If you have been physically or emotionally wounded in the past, you are not ready to get married until you have dealt with these issues head on and received healing in these areas.

You shouldn't enter into marriage while making excuses for not being healed from your past. The man at the pool of Bethesda had an infir-

---

[4] Encarta Webster's Dictionary of the English Language, 2nd ed., S.V. "hole."

mity. When he was confronted by Jesus, he made excuses about why he had not been made whole. He blamed others for not helping him. Yet, Jesus did not entertain these excuses—He just spoke directly to the problem!

The woman with the issue of blood had made up her mind that she would be whole when she touched the hem of Jesus' garment. She risked being exposed and possibly stoned in order to receive her healing. We must not let fear of what people may say or fear of exposing our true feelings stop us from receiving our healing. Romans 8:1-2 tells us that if we walk after the Spirit, we are made free from the condemnation that comes from being ruled by our flesh. *"There is therefore now no condemnation to them which are in Christ Jesus, who walk not after the flesh, but after the Spirit."*[5] It is the law of sin and death that would keep us in bondage to our feelings and hold us captive to our past. *"Stand fast therefore in the liberty wherewith Christ hath made us free, and be not entangled again with the yoke of bondage."*[6] Ask the Holy Spirit to help you root out any holes in your life. When you discover a hole, don't try to hide it, instead be willing to seek help. Ask God for an accountability partner. This person could be a pastor, a spiritually strong friend or family member, an elder who has the wisdom of God, or a counselor. Jesus said that He was *"...anointed to preach the gospel to the poor; to heal the broken hearted, to preach deliverance to the captives, and recovering of sight to the blind, to set at liberty them that are bruised."*[7] Here we see the will of God concerning our wholeness.

We believe the reason so many marriages end in divorce is because the holes in the lives of many couples have never been dealt with. Don't let loneliness stop you from completing the process of your wholeness. This process will take time and requires patience. *"But let patience have*

---

[5]Romans 8:1 KJV
[6]Galatians 5:1 KJV
[7]Luke 4:18 KJV

her perfect work, that ye may be perfect and entire, wanting nothing."[8]

THE HEALING PROCESS

The healing process begins by building a strong relationship with God. We must first get a revelation of God's love in order to receive the healing that He purchased for us through His Son Jesus. Let us examine what the God kind of love looks like. In order to understand God's love, we must study I Corinthians the 13th chapter. Years ago while meditating on this chapter, the Lord revealed to me that no weapon formed against love can prosper. This helped me understand why some Christians were wounded and seemed to be open to the attacks of the enemy. When we walk in the God kind of love and overcome evil with good, the love of God acts as a shield over our heart that protects us from being wounded or overcome by the evil acts of others.

God's love never strikes out or even takes into account a suffered wrong. God's love does not make an excuse for a suffered wrong; it covers it. Love covers a multitude of sins. We must not equate the God kind of love with natural human love or an emotional experience. Natural human love is dependent on how well someone treats us or what they do for us. Godly love, agape, is not based on how it is treated. God's love for us does not depend on what we do, but on who He is. God is love. Even in our condition of brokenness, God loved us enough to pay the ultimate price for us to be His own.

In Acts 6:8-15 and Acts chapter 7, we see an example of the God kind of love through the life of Stephen. Stephen was full of the Spirit and was speaking the truth in love. The people resisted the truth of God's Word spoken through Stephen and stoned him. Even at the point of death, Stephen prayed and asked God not to charge the people with this sin of murder. This may seem like an extreme example of the love of God

---

[8]James 1:4 KJV

in action, but it is the same example of love God expressed when He gave His Son's life in exchange for our salvation. Most of us will not be required to lay down our physical lives, but we are called to die to our fleshly desires. Who would have thought that the way to be healed is to die? *"I am crucified with Christ: nevertheless I live; yet not I, but Christ lives in me: and the life which I now live in the flesh I live by the faith of the Son of God, who loved me, and gave himself for me."[9]* We will discuss the different types of love in another chapter.

Forgiveness is the key to releasing the hurt of the past and being made free. In Matthew 6:14-15, the Word of God tells us that we must forgive those who have trespassed against us, in order to receive forgiveness from God for our own trespasses. This act of forgiving others is a choice. It is not based on whether the person is worthy or even acknowledges his or her trespass. One of the dictionary's definitions of trespass is to commit an offense or sin.[10] Forgiveness means to cease to blame or feel resentment about an offense or offender. Forgiveness means to cancel or let off a debt or debtor.[11] When we recognize that God has cancelled our debt of sin through the sacrifice of His Son, then we should be willing to follow the same example of forgiveness toward others. *"And be ye kind one to another, tender-hearted, forgiving one another, even as God for Christ's sake hath forgiven you."[12] "Forbearing one another, and forgiving one another, if any man have a quarrel against any: even as Christ forgave you, so also do ye."[13]*

God knows that when we won't forgive others, we are held captive to our feelings of offense and cannot experience the freedom of forgiveness. We give the offender control over our lives. When we walk in

---

[9]Galatians 2:20 KJV
[10]The Random House Dictionary Concise Edition – s.v. "trespass"
[11]The Random House Dictionary Concise Edition – s.v. "forgive"
[12]Ephesians 4:32 KJV
[13]Colossians 3:13 KJV
[15]Hebrews 12:14-15 AMP

unforgiveness, we relive the hurt of the past and allow it to control how we relate to others in the present. Just as Stephen forgave the people who stoned him and prayed that God would not charge them with the sin of murder, we must pray for the people in our lives who have mistreated or abused us.

"Strive to live in peace with everybody and pursue that consecration and holiness without which no one will [ever] see the Lord. Exercise foresight and be on the watch to look [after one another], to see that no one falls back from and fails to secure God's grace (His unmerited favor and spiritual blessing), in order that no root of resentment (rancor, bitterness, or hatred) shoots forth and causes trouble and bitter torment, and the many become contaminated and defiled by it."[15]

Many people are experiencing the results of a root of bitterness that has been in their family for generations, unforgiveness that goes back so far that no one even remembers what started it. This has caused a generational curse to be passed on. God, through Jesus, has set us free from generational curses. We must walk in love and forgiveness in order to break free from the root of bitterness.

Romans 12:17-21 tells us:

3. Do not repay evil with evil.

4. Be honest and above reproach with everyone.

5. As far as it depends on you, live at peace with everyone.

6. Leave the way open for God's wrath.

Forgiving others is an act of faith in God, not in man. Don't let your feelings get the best of you. Forgiving others does not immediately release you from feelings of hurt, but it starts the healing process. Remember, forgiving someone does not mean that you open yourself up to continued abuse. In some instances, you may need to end the relationship with the person who is responsible for the abuse.

Examine your own life to determine if you have become the abuser. We must acknowledge our own sins and be quick to ask forgiveness from others. Accountability is important. Being accountable to someone who will encourage you to obey God's Word and pray for you is essential to your spiritual growth and maturity—someone you can trust to speak the truth in love and help you get free from the abuser or abusive behavior.

ACHIEVING WHOLENESS

Whole - *comprising the full quantity, amount, or extent. Containing all the elements properly belonging. Not cut up or divided. Uninjured, undamaged, or unbroken. Healthy or sound. Math, not fractional. All the amount or every part of something. A thing complete in itself.*[14]

Jesus said *"...If ye continue in my word, then are ye my disciples indeed; And ye shall know the truth, and the truth shall make you free."*[15] Now that you have heard the Word of God concerning love, you must continue in that Word in order to be made free from all the wounds and condemnation of the past. When you meditate on God's Word, it will bring freedom in your life.

In Luke 17:12-19, Jesus heals the ten lepers but only one returns to worship Him and give Him thanks. The one who returned was a Samaritan. Jesus asked where the other nine were. Jesus turned to the Samaritan who had been healed and said *"Arise, go thy way; thy faith hath made thee whole."*[16] Here we see that even though all of the lepers were healed, only one was made **whole**. This was a direct result of his wor-

[14] The Random House Dictionary Concise Edition s.v. "whole."
[15] John 8:31-32 KJV
[16] Luke 17:19 KJV

ship and giving glory to God for his healing. Jesus told him that his faith had made him **whole**. This state of wholeness brought him to complete restoration of all things that were missing or broken in his body. While the other nine were healed and the leprosy left their bodies, they were still not **whole** because they did not receive the restoration of their flesh or missing body parts. What a great lesson this is to all believers who want to receive restoration and wholeness in their lives. We must be willing to give God the glory for every healing and victory we achieve in our lives as a direct result of receiving the Word of God on love, peace, the fruit of the Spirit, and other subjects. In this way, we show our faith in God. Then with thanksgiving, we take hold of our complete healing and restoration that Jesus purchased for us.

Our relationship with God will enable us to keep the place of wholeness that we have received by faith. *"Stand fast therefore in the liberty where-with Christ hath made us free, and be not entangled again with the yoke of bondage."*[17] In the previous chapter, Paul is referring to the natural or the "flesh," and the supernatural or the "spirit." He states that we should no longer identify ourselves as slaves to the flesh, or in bondage to our flesh. Man is a three part being—he is a spirit, he possesses a soul, and he lives in a body. The flesh refers to our body or the five human senses: sight, hearing, smell, taste and touch. The spirit refers to the heart of man as the life God breathed into man at creation. Man's conscience is the voice of man's spirit. The scripture also refers to the spirit of man as the candle of the Lord. Through prayer and meditation of God's Word, we change and influence the condition of our soul, or mind, will, and emotions. Paul refers to this as the three part nature of man in I Thessalonians 5:23, *"...I pray God your whole spirit and soul and body be preserved blameless unto the coming our Lord Jesus Christ."*[18]

Psalm 1:1-3 gives us a guideline to achieve spiritual maturity and

[17]Galatians 5:1 KJV
[18]I Thessalonians 5:23 KJV

wholeness:

- You will be blessed when you do not walk in the counsel or follow the advice of the ungodly or stand subjected to the ways or paths of sinners, nor sit down or relax and rest or become comfortable where the scornful and the mockers gather.

- Delight in the law of the Lord (Word of God); and meditate in the precepts instructions and teachings of God day and night.

- As a result of meditating on the Word, you will be like a tree firmly planted and tended by the rivers of water that brings forth its fruit in its season; your leaf (life) also will not wither and whatever you do will prosper and you will come to a place of maturity.

After we have experienced the love of God and know what it feels like to receive unconditional love, we have what it takes to experience wholeness in all our relationships.

CHAPTER 2

GOD'S DESIGN FOR MARRIAGE

Marriage is a covenant that God created between one man and one woman.

> *"The LORD God said, 'It is not good for the man to be alone. I will make a helper suitable for him.' Now the LORD God had formed out of the ground all the beasts of the field and all the birds of the air. He brought them to the man to see what he would name them; and whatever the man called each living creature, that was its name. So the man gave names to all the livestock, the birds of the air and all the beasts of the field. But for Adam no suitable helper was found. So the LORD God caused the man to fall into a deep sleep; and while he was sleeping, he took one of the man's ribs and closed up the place with flesh. Then the LORD God made a woman from the rib he had taken out of the man, and he brought her to the man. The man said, 'This is now bone of my bones and flesh of my flesh; she shall be called "woman," for she was taken out of man.' For this reason a man will leave his father and mother and be united to his wife, and they will become one flesh."*[19]

The first marriage ceremony was when God brought woman to man. God was a representation of the father of the bride. As the Father of us all, He gave woman to man in marriage.

The covenant of marriage is reflected in the covenant between God and

---

[19]Genesis 2:18-24 NIV

Abraham recorded in Genesis 17:2-11. In that covenant, there was a pledge or promise made between God and Abraham. God promised to make Abraham the father of many nations, yet at this time Abraham had no children and was ninety-nine years old. The conditions of the covenant were that Abraham would circumcise all the males born in his house, even his servants. God called this an everlasting covenant, which meant it was not to be broken. In the same way, God called man and woman into covenant with each other.

The marriage covenant begins with the wedding vows—promises made between the bride and groom. It is important to include scriptures in the wedding vows such as those mentioned in this chapter, because the Word of God is a sure foundation on which to build the covenant of your marriage. The seal of this covenant is the joining of husband and wife in sexual unity on the wedding day in the marriage bed. God intended for the husband and wife to be joined together in spirit, soul and body. God intended the marriage between man and woman to be permanent, or till death do they part, as seen in Mark 10:9: *"What therefore God has united (joined together), let not man separate or divide."*[20]

Woman was made *from* man *for* man. Woman is a gift *from* God *to* man. God brought the woman to Adam and he received her and said, *"This creature is now bone of my bones and flesh of my flesh; she shall be called Woman, because she was taken out of a man."*[21] Adam called the woman "bone of my bones and flesh of my flesh," signifying how close the relationship between a husband and wife was meant to be. God revealed His intention for marriage—the union of two becoming one—when He used the rib of man to create woman.

"He who finds a wife finds a good thing, and obtains favor from the LORD."[22]

---

[20]Mark 10:9 AMP
[21]Genesis 2:23 AMP
[22]Proverbs 18:22 NKJV

The marriage relationship was meant to be the closest relationship created by God, outside of our relationship with Him. Jesus repeats a portion of Genesis 2:24 in Matthew 19:5-6, *"For this reason a man shall leave behind his father and his mother and be joined to his wife and cleave closely to her permanently, And the two shall become one flesh, so that they are no longer two, but one flesh. What therefore God has united (joined together), let not man separate or divide."[23]* Just like God made Eve to be a suitable mate for Adam and brought her to him, He also has a suitable mate for you and will lead you to him or her at the right time.

LEAVE

Leave - *to go away or depart. To stop, cease, abandon or exclude.[24]*

In order to truly cleave to your mate, you must first leave all others behind. This includes parents, as stated in Mark 10:7. One of the biggest problems with many marriages is that the husband or wife has never really left parents, family or friends, which means they are not able to put a priority on their relationship with their spouse. This may be difficult depending on a person's culture, family background and experience. We encourage couples to spend a majority of their time apart from family and friends for the first six months to a year of their marriage so they can focus on each other and begin to cleave. *"When a man is newly married, he shall not go out with the army or be charged with any business; he shall be free at home one year and shall cheer his wife whom he has taken."[25]*

The leaving process should begin prior to marriage, when a young man or woman grows up and begins to experience independence from his or her parents. They need to begin to take on more and more of the

---

[23]Matthew 19:5-6 AMP - (author's paraphrase)
[24]The Random House Dictionary Concise Edition 1989, s.v. "leave".
[25]Deuteronomy 24:5 AMP

responsibility for their own lives and decisions. Parents need to release their children over a process of time as they grow into adulthood. This is not an easy process for many families, but it is important for the growth and development of the child into a man or woman. Some of you may have been taking care of yourself for a long time, so this may not be a hard process for you. However, this may be a problem for your potential mate, depending on his or her family makeup.

Parents should not have the financial responsibility for their children after they leave home. Money should not be used as a way to control your children. This means letting them pay their own bills and buy their own clothes, cars, and other things. This is how children learn to become responsible for themselves and gain their independence. Parents should become mentors and advisers to their children after they leave home and/or get married.[26] Parents should not be dictators or try to manipulate their children and keep them from cleaving to their spouse.

It is important for men and women to seek the blessing of their parents when choosing a mate. One reason children should seek their parents' blessing on who they are to marry is because their parents will ultimately be affected by their decision. Long after you have left your parents' home, there will still be a spiritual and emotional connection between you. Even though you will start a new family, your parents' role will change and they will become mentors to you and possibly to your children. Your parents should have a unique view of who you are and desire to see you choose a mate who is suitable for you. They love you and want the best for you. If you have spiritual parents, they are looking at your potential mate to see how you fit each other's spiritual growth, maturity and calling. It's important to seek wise counsel prior to marriage if your parents are not involved in your life.

---

[26]Proverbs 4:1-7 KJV

CLEAVE

Cleave - *to cling, stick, stay close, cleave, keep close, stick to, stick with, follow closely, join to, overtake, catch.*[27] *To cling closely, steadfastly, or faithfully to somebody or something.*[28]

It is important for a new couple not to live with their parents and if possible, live a good distance away so they will not be tempted to run to their parents in times of disagreement. It is during these times of disagreement that a couple learns how to work through differences and begin to cleave. Never involve your parents or family in your disagreements. This will only cause them to have trouble accepting your mate in the future. They will still remember the disagreement long after you and your spouse have made up and are over your difficulties. Always present a united front before family and friends. Never use words like, *He wanted to do this,* or *She didn't want to do that,* in front of them. Instead, use statements like, *We decided to do or not to do this or that.*

When dealing with disagreements, pray and acknowledge God's Word. The Word of God has an answer for every situation you will ever face. Even though there is no scripture telling you when to buy a car or house, there is scripture regarding being led by peace and not walking in strife. We encourage couples to meditate on I Corinthians the 13th chapter, which shows us how to walk in love and not be selfish. It is important to operate in the fruit of the Spirit.[29] Remember, how much you love God and have experienced His love for you is how much you will love your mate.

Cleaving is a process of transforming our thinking to consider our mates and put their needs first. It takes a servant attitude like Jesus <u>demonstrated</u>. He put our need for salvation ahead of His own life. He

[27]Strong's Expanded Dictionary of Bible Words, s.v. "cleave."
[28]Encarta Webster's Dictionary of the English Language, s.v. "cleave."
[29]Galatians 5:22-26 KJV

laid down His life for His friends, and He has called us to lay down our lives for each other and for the gospel. *"Greater love hath no man than this, that a man lay down his life for his friends."[30]*

Cleaving involves the spirit, soul and body. The process of cleaving in spirit begins when you begin to pray together and have times of devotion before God. Your spirits become united as one in purpose and pursuit toward God. It is important to take the time to discuss the call of God on your lives. During times of prayer and worship before God, you should exercise the spiritual gifts God has placed in each of you. When you begin to flow together in spiritual oneness, you will be able to walk in unity and agreement. The soul already began the process of cleaving during the friendship stage of your relationship. Then it grew stronger during the engagement stage and will continue to bond in marriage as you maintain good communication, sexual unity and have recreational time together. After marriage, the body should be the last to cleave through touching and sexual unity.

---

[30]John 15:13 KJV

CHAPTER 3

BUILDING A STRONG FOUNDATION
(LOVE)

"Therefore be imitators of God [copy Him and follow His example], as well-beloved children [imitate their father]. And walk in love, [esteeming and delighting in one another] as Christ loved us and gave Himself up for us, a slain offering and sacrifice to God [for you, so that it became] a sweet fragrance." [31]

It is our desire to be imitators of God. In order to do this, we must start by walking in love. God is love, and we have the love of God in us if we are His children. When we accepted Jesus as our Savior and Lord, the love of God came to dwell inside of us in the person of the Holy Spirit. Understanding the love God has for us and experiencing that unconditional love helps prepare us for the unconditional love that is required in all our relationships, especially marriage. Developing the love of God in us requires spending time meditating on God's Word. That is why it is so important to read scriptures like I Corinthians the 13th chapter and Ephesians 5:1-2 and meditate on them continually. We learn the ways of God and see His love expressed throughout both the Old and New Testaments.

In previous chapters, we have mentioned I Corinthians the 13th chapter. We want to take the time now to apply this scripture as the basis for a successful marriage. The Apostle Paul devoted a whole chapter to describing the God kind of love, and we would like to devote this chapter

---

[31]Ephesians 5:1-2 AMP

to explaining how this love will create an unbreakable foundation on which you can build your marriage.

The love of God is a sacrificial love that keeps on giving without expecting anything in return. This is in total opposition to everything we see in the world today. But remember, we are *in* this world but we are not *of* this world. This means that we don't live our lives according to the same standards of the world. The world's way of love is based on feelings and is not motivated by the spirit. As believers, we are to be motivated by the Spirit of God and not by the dictates of our flesh. The flesh will never be satisfied until it is in subjection, or made to submit, to the Word of God. As Paul said, *"For the flesh lusteth against the Spirit, and the Spirit against the flesh: and these are contrary the one to the other: so that ye cannot do the things that ye would. But if ye be led of the Spirit, ye are not under the law."* [32] We are not teaching you to be under condemnation to the law, but rather to be led by the Spirit. Paul also said, *"I am crucified with Christ: nevertheless I live; yet not I, but Christ liveth in me: and the life which I now live in the flesh I live by the faith of the Son of God, who loved me, and gave himself for me."* [33] When we walk in the Spirit, we are able to walk in God's love because *"the fruit of the Spirit is love, joy, peace, longsuffering, gentleness, goodness, faith, meekness, temperance..."* [34] *And they that are Christ's have crucified the flesh with the affections and lusts. If we live in the Spirit, let us also walk in the Spirit.* [35] We cannot make excuses for yielding to our flesh, but rather we must be willing to put the flesh to death by submitting to the love of God.

Love is an action word so it must be expressed by demonstration. *"But whoso hath this world's good, and seeth his brother have need, and shutteth up his bowels of compassion from him, how dwelleth the love of God*

---

[32]Galatians 5:17-18 KJV
[33]Galatians 2:20 KJV
[34]Galatians 5:22-23 KJV
[35]Galatians 5:24-25 KJV

in him? My little children, let us not love in word, neither in tongue; but in deed and in truth."[36]

There are five Greek words used to describe the different ways to express love:

1. **Epithumia** - to have a strong desire for someone or something.

2. **Eros** - romance, or the emotional expression of love.

3. **Storge** - the love between family members.

4. **Philae** - the concept of friendship and companionship (brotherly love).

5. **Agape** - the highest form of love, which is supernatural and unconditional.

All five of these expressions of love will play a role in the development of your relationship with your potential mate. During the friendship stage of your relationship when you start talking and finding out what each other likes, you will experience different levels of these expressions of love, such as phileo. Then as the relationship grows and you begin to express your love for each other, you will most likely end up in eros. This will turn into epithumia as you desire to be with each other more and more. But agape can only be expressed by someone who has experienced this kind of unconditional love. Believers who have experienced and understand the love God has for them and have developed a love for Him that's not based on how good they are but on how good He is, can fully express agape love toward others.

Let's take another look at I Corinthians the 13th chapter:

> *"If I speak in the tongues of men and of angels, but have not love, I am only a resounding gong or a clanging cymbal.*

[36] I John 3:17-18 KJV

If I have the gift of prophecy and can fathom all myster-
ies and all knowledge, and if I have a faith that can move
mountains, but have not love, I am nothing. If I give all I
possess to the poor and surrender my body to the flames,
but have not love, I gain nothing."[37]

In this above passage of scripture, we see that no spiritual gift or self-less, sacrificial act can compare to the expression of God's agape love. This love is not based on works, but just like faith, our love requires expression through corresponding actions such as those listed in the next portion of the passage.

"Love is patient, love is kind. It does not envy, it does not
boast, it is not proud. It is not rude, it is not self-seeking,
it is not easily angered, it keeps no record of wrongs. Love
does not delight in evil but rejoices with the truth. It always
protects, always trusts, always hopes, always perseveres.
Love never fails. But where there are prophecies, they will
cease; where there are tongues, they will be stilled; where
there is knowledge, it will pass away. For we know in part
and we prophesy in part, but when perfection comes, the
imperfect disappears."[38]

- God's love is immutable, it never changes because it is not based on feelings.[39]

- God's love is indestructible, it never fails, and cannot be

---

[37]I Corinthians 13:1-3 NIV
[38]I Corinthians 13:4-10 NIV
[39]Hebrews 6:18 NKJV

overcome by the evil acts of others. [40]

- God's love is inexhaustible, it never runs out, gives up or quits.[41]

---

[40]I Corinthians 13:8 AMP
[41]Matthew 18:22 AMP

Before and After

CHAPTER 4

COMPATIBILITY

"Do not be unequally yoked together with unbelievers. For what fellowship has righteousness with lawlessness? And what communion has light with darkness? And what accord has Christ with Belial? Or what part has a believer with an unbeliever?" [42]

There are signs of incompatibility that should not be overlooked when choosing a mate. We will call these signs of incompatibility "red lights." These red lights are major disagreements that have not been resolved, yet should not be ignored. Being unequally yoked with an unbeliever, not agreeing on where you will live or what ministry you are called to or whether you want children and/or when you want to start a family, are some common red lights. These red lights should be discussed and resolved during the friendship stage of your relationship. Many couples have run these red lights and warning signals in their relationships, ultimately leading to breakup or divorce.

Compatible - *capable of existing together in harmony.* [43]

We are not supposed to try to change our mates to be more like us. We should appreciate the differences they bring to the relationship. During the friendship stage of the relationship, we tend to be drawn to the differences of the other person's personality. While that is one of

---

[42]II Corinthians 6:14-15 NJKV
[43]The Random House Dictionary Concise Edition, s.v. "compatible."

the things that made them stand out from among others, this personality difference will cause problems after the marriage if we don't learn how to accept their differences. It is important to take the time to ask questions to find out more about what you have in common, or what makes you compatible.

As II Corinthians 6:14-15 states, you must first find out if this person is born again. This doesn't mean that they just go to church or believe in God. It is important to find out their testimony. What has their relationship with God been like? How did they come to the realization that they needed Jesus as their Savior? Then find out what spiritual level they are on and how often they read the Bible and pray. Do they attend church? If so, how often and where? Are they involved in ministry at their church?

COMMITMENT TO SEXUAL PURITY

"For you know what charges and precepts we gave you [on the authority and by the inspiration of] the Lord Jesus. For this is the will of God, that you should be consecrated (separated and set apart for pure and holy living): that you should abstain and shrink from all sexual vice, that each one of you should know how to possess (control, manage) his own body in consecration (purity, separated from things profane) and honor, not [to be used] in the passion of lust like the heathen, who are ignorant of the true God and have no knowledge of His will, that no man transgress and overreach his brother and defraud him in this matter or defraud his brother in business. For the Lord is an avenger in all these things, as we have already warned you solemnly and told you plainly. For God has not called us to impurity but to consecration [to dedicate ourselves to the most thorough purity]. Therefore whoever disregards (sets aside and rejects this) disregards not man but God, Whose [very] Spirit [Whom] He

gives to you is holy (chaste, pure)." [44]

You may ask why is it important not to have sex before marriage. This scripture says that we must exercise control over our body and mind by keeping them under the control of our newly created spirit. Lack of self control is a sin that overtakes our will and leads to no restraint. There is no way to satisfy this form of lust. Our minds must be renewed by the Word of God concerning sexual purity. The Bible calls sex before marriage fornication, and we must have the same mind which is in Christ. We must not follow the same example of the world. We must make a commitment to sexual purity out of our love for God.

We can cause our potential mate to sin by defrauding him/her due to our lack of self control. Touching inappropriately, kissing, hugging, or dressing in a revealing way are things that can lead to sex outside of marriage. *"If then you were raised with Christ, seek those things which are above, where Christ is, sitting at the right hand of God. Set your mind on things above, not on things on the earth. For you died, and your life is hidden with Christ in God. When Christ who is our life appears, then you also will appear with Him in glory. Therefore put to death your members which are on the earth: fornication, uncleanness, passion, evil desire, and covetousness, which is idolatry. Because of these things the wrath of God is coming upon the sons of disobedience, in which you yourselves once walked when you lived in them."* [45] The Bible says that these things cause the wrath of God to come on the children of disobedience. Our flesh will lead us to do what pleases us but our spirit will lead us to do what pleases God. When we crucify the flesh and deny its power to control us, we will be able to walk in God's love and reach maturity in our love toward our mate.

Galatians 5:13-26 tells us that we have been called to freedom, but we

---

[44] I Thessalonians 4:2-8 AMP
[45] Colossians 3:1-7 NKJV

must not use our freedom to satisfy the lusts of our flesh or as an excuse for selfishness. Many people have a problem living according to the spirit because they are carnal and have not put their spirit before the desires of their flesh. This scripture tells us that the flesh is in opposition to the Spirit of God; they are in constant conflict with each other. Many Christians have not resolved the conflict of their flesh warring against their spirit. Just because our flesh desires to do something, doesn't mean that it is okay to do it if it's in opposition to the Word of God. Just because a person is born again does not mean that he or she is spiritual. We can see this in the Corinthian church when Paul wrote the letter to them urging them not to be carnal or ruled by their flesh (II Corinthians 10:3-7). If your potential mate is led by the flesh now, he or she will be led by the flesh in marriage.

Submitting is the link in the chain of God's divine order: Jesus submits to the Father, the husband submits to Jesus, and the wife submits to the husband. The children learn how to submit to their parents by the example of their parents' submission to God and to each other.[46] Women are called to submit to their husbands, but if the husband is not yielded to the Spirit of God, he is not going to be the right leader for the household. He must first be submitted to God, walking in the love of God. He must be an example by the love that he shows toward his wife. Men should look for a woman who is submitted to God because if she is not submitted to God, she will not be able to submit to the leadership of her husband. We realize that submission seems like a dirty word in our society, but remember we are *in* this world but we are not *of* this world. We are not talking about someone putting you in a choke hold and making you submit—but by love **serve** one another.

Another area of compatibility involves the different backgrounds of the husband and wife—how they were raised. An only child will have a dif-

---

[46]Ephesians 5:21-26; 6:1-3 KJV

ferent outlook and different experiences than someone who was born in a large family with eight brothers and sisters. Did your family show emotion with kisses and hugs, or were they reserved? Were you raised in a Christian home? Were your parents committed to their marriage or are they divorced? What is your family's attitude toward your prospective mate? Are you close to your family? How much time do you plan on spending with them after the marriage? Do you like each other's friends? Your mate's attitude toward money and spending habits come from his or her family's attitude toward finances. Are they a spend thrift or an emotional spender? Do they have a savings account? Do they pay tithes? What role will TV have in your home? How do you plan to spend your free time? What will the division of labor be around your home? Will the wife work outside the home after you have children? These questions and more should be asked and answered satisfactorily before you consider this person as a potential mate.

"Wherefore henceforth know we no man after the flesh: yea, though we have known Christ after the flesh, yet now henceforth know we him no more."[47] The word of God admonishes us to know no man after the flesh, because the real you is not your flesh, it's your spirit (heart). *"But, on the contrary, as the Scripture says, What eye has not seen and ear has not heard and has not entered into the heart of man, [all that] God has prepared (made and keeps ready) for those who love Him [who hold Him in affectionate reverence, promptly obeying Him and gratefully recognizing the benefits He has bestowed]. Yet to us God has unveiled and revealed them by and through His Spirit, for the [Holy] Spirit searches diligently, exploring and examining everything, even sounding the profound and bottomless things of God [the divine counsels and things hidden and beyond man's scrutiny]. For what person perceives (knows and understands) what passes through a man's thoughts except the man's own spirit within him? Just so no one discerns (comes to know and comprehend) the thoughts of God*

---

[47] II Corinthians 5:16 KJV

except the Spirit of God."[48]

This scripture reveals what it means to know someone by the spirit. Take the time to find out how your prospective mate thinks. What motivates him or her? It is important to examine the lifestyle of your potential mate and get to know the hidden man of the heart.[49] There is too much focus on the outward appearance of man, instead of the inward man. It takes time to get to know the real person on the inside so don't rush into marriage with a stranger. Take time to be friends and spend time getting to know each other without the pressure of trying to be a couple. Your friendship should be allowed to develop naturally so if this person is a potential mate, it will become evident by the closeness and compatibility you both experience. Just because a person is a Christian doesn't mean he or she is the right person for you. You must find out what the spiritual calling of your potential mate is and if it is compatible to what God has called you to do. The longer the friendship, the stronger the relationship will be after the marriage. You find out things about each other during the friendship stage. Walls also begin to come down during this stage. There is no threat of a breakup. You are free to be yourself. This causes greater understanding and lessens the chance of being unequally yoked.

The marriage between a husband and wife is both spiritual and natural. That is why it is so important to get to know the person you are considering as a potential mate by the spirit first. Remember, Jesus was *all* God and *all* man, but He knew how to balance the spiritual with the natural. Jesus met the natural needs of the people who followed Him into a deserted area where there was no place to buy food. He had the disciples sit the people down and then when they found food, He blessed it and gave it to His disciples to give to the people to eat so they would not faint on their way back home. We cannot be so heavenly minded

[48] I Corinthians 2:9-11 AMP
[49] I Peter 3:4 KJV

40

that we are no earthly good! We must recognize that there must be a balance of the spiritual and natural coming together to make our marriage unified.

Each time you get together, pray with each other and begin to build your relationship around your love for God. Take time to talk about what you believe the call of God is for your life. The Bible tells us to know no man after the flesh. This means that we cannot purely use natural human understanding and reasoning when we are getting to know our potential mate. What looks good and seems right is not necessarily the right choice. Remember, when God chose David to be king, he was the most unlikely choice. He was not big and strong like some of his other brothers and seemed small and unqualified by natural standards. He was a shepherd. He was more comfortable with animals than with people. However, God looked at David's heart and how he honored God above man. We must get to know the heart of our potential mate. How much does he or she love God? Remember, how much your mate loves God is how much he or she will be able to love you.

"But seek first the kingdom of God and His righteousness, and all these things shall be added to you."[50] Don't make the mistake of only looking for the right person, prepare yourself to be the right person for the mate God has for you. Let God lead you to the person He wants you to marry.

FINDING YOUR PERSONALITY TYPE

Take a personality test to find out what your potential mate's personality type is. There are several different personality tests out there so it is a good idea to take more than one test. This will help you understand how you and your mate think, helping you communicate better. Most people are drawn to someone who has a different personality type than their own. However, lack of understanding about the differences in

[50]Matthew 6:33 NKJV

4

your personalities can cause a lot of friction in your relationship and even lead to divorce.

Remember that your personality type is not an excuse for disobeying the Word of God or not walking in the love of God toward your mate. Learn to balance the hard and soft sides of love. If you or your spouse do not know how to operate in these types of love, there will be disagreements. The hard side of love is correction, discipline, and confrontation, while the soft side of love is tender, sensitive, compassionate, and forgiving. Jesus was a perfect balance of every personality type. He was decisive and took charge when He went through the temple and cleared out the money changers.[51] He was sociable and popular at the wedding feast when He turned the water into wine,[52] and when He ate with sinners.[53] He was disciplined and loyal as He fulfilled the law and did only what the Father told Him to do.[54] He was nurturing and compassionate toward the people and He healed them.[55]

We want to once again encourage you and your mate to have accountability partners who can speak into your lives and help you work on any personality problems. When God shows you an area of your personality that is out of balance with His Word, work on it and let your mate or your accountability partner hold you accountable. Remember, the Word of God has instructions on how we are to treat one another, loving our neighbor as ourselves and submitting to one another in the fear of God.

---

[51]Matthew 21:10-13 KJV
[52]John 2:1-9 KJV
[53]Matthew 11:19 KJV
[54]Matthew 5:17 & John 8:28-29 KJV
[55]Matthew 9:36 & Matthew 14:14 KJV

Chapter 5

ROLES IN MARRIAGE

"And further, submit to one another out of reverence for Christ. For wives, this means submit to your husbands as to the Lord. For a husband is the head of his wife as Christ is the head of the church. He is the Savior of his body, the church. As the church submits to Christ, so you wives should submit to your husbands in everything. For husbands, this means love your wives, just as Christ loved the church. He gave up his life for her to make her holy and clean, washed by the cleansing of God's word. He did this to present her to himself as a glorious church without a spot or wrinkle or any other blemish. Instead, she will be holy and without fault. In the same way, husbands ought to love their wives as they love their own bodies. For a man who loves his wife actually shows love for himself. No one hates his own body but feeds and cares for it, just as Christ cares for the church. And we are members of his body. As the Scriptures say, 'A man leaves his father and mother and is joined to his wife, and the two are united into one.' This is a great mystery, but it is an illustration of the way Christ and the church are one. So again I say, each man must love his wife as he loves himself, and the wife must respect her husband."[56]

---

[56]Ephesians 5:21-33 NLT

The relationship between the husband and wife should be a reflection of the relationship between Christ and the church. Jesus said that He came not to be ministered to but to minister and to give His life as a ransom. The husband is to be like Christ and the wife is to be like the church. Love is always giving, not expecting to receive anything in return. The husband is always giving; he is a servant leader. The wife is a receiver, always reflecting what the husband is giving. If the husband is giving out love, the wife will reflect love back to him but if he is giving out hatred, bitterness or strife, this is what the wife will reflect back to him.

Jesus did not yield to the flesh nor did He yield to the will of the people. He only yielded to the will of the Father. We are also called to yield to God, not our flesh. We should not be moved to respond in the flesh when our spouse is not walking in love toward us.

THE HUSBAND'S ROLE

"But God demonstrates His own love toward us, in that while we were still sinners, Christ died for us."[57] In the same way, husbands are to demonstrate their love for their wives through unconditional love. The husband is called to serve, even as Jesus served His disciples at the last supper. In the same manner that Jesus washed the disciples feet, the husband is to wash his wife with the Word of God.

- The husband should demonstrate God's love toward his wife.

- The husband should keep God first in his life.

- The husband should lead in prayer. He should keep the Word before his eyes.

- The husband should speak God's Word over his wife.

---

[57]Romans 5:8 NKJV

- The husband should be the first to leave his father and mother in order to prepare for marriage.

- The husband should be the leader in hearing God's direction for his household. Just like Jesus led by demonstrating the fruit of the Spirit and the gifts of the Spirit, so the husband should be a leader in the things of the Spirit.

Men must know how to balance the things of the spirit and the things of the flesh. He must know when his wife needs his ear or shoulder, not just an answer. Men are problem solvers and tend to try to resolve a problem when their wives bring something to their attention. However, a wife just usually needs to vent or verbalize her feelings, without wanting a solution. Remember, Jesus was *all* God and *all* man, but He knew how to be touched with the feelings of our infirmities. He also knew when it was time to get alone in prayer. Likewise, husbands must know when to give their wives attention and affection. They should also know how to take their wives' needs to the Lord in prayer.

When Adam saw the serpent speaking to Eve, he should have stepped in as his wife's protector and taken authority over the serpent. Adam could have commanded the serpent to leave because he was the god of this world. The husband is supposed to be his wife's protector, even as Christ gave His life for the church.

The husband should not take advantage of his wife through physical or emotional abuse. The Scripture tells the husband to love his wife even as he loves himself. This may cause a problem if he doesn't love himself. That is why it is important to be whole from any wounds of the past before entering into marriage. In Genesis the 3rd chapter, after Adam sinned, God came into the garden and called Adam saying, "Where art thou?" Adam heard the voice of God and hid himself. When God confronted him about his sin, Adam accused the woman saying, "the woman whom thou gavest to be with me, she gave me of the tree, and I did eat."[58] The husband should not blame his wife, but rather cover his wife. Adam should not have made an excuse for his sin; he should have protected his wife and admitted to his sin. By doing so, he would have covered his wife.

How much you love God is how much you will love your spouse. That love needs to be kept strong and fresh. You need to continue to have date nights, gifts and surprises. Keep in contact with each other throughout the day through phone calls, emails, text, and other means. Take time for intimate conversation. Let your wife know what's going on at work. Value your wife's opinion, recognizing that God has given her insight. Remember, the husband is not a dictator. He's a servant leader. Build your wife up around others, complimenting her. Admit when you have been wrong. Don't make plans without your wife or correct her in public. Your wife is not your daughter; she is your helpmate. Don't compare her to other women.

THE WIFE'S ROLE

"Wives, be subject (be submissive and adapt yourselves) to your own husbands as [a service] to the Lord. For the husband is head of the wife as Christ is the Head of the church, Himself the Savior of [His] body. As the church is subject to Christ, so let wives also be subject in everything to their husbands."[59]

The wife is called to submit to her husband as the church is called to submit to Christ in all things. The wife is not to have a separate identity and/or separate agenda from her husband. The wife is expected to represent her husband, walk in unity with him, and submit to his direction as he submits to Christ. Jesus stated that if we loved Him, we would

[58]Genesis 3:12 KJV
[59]Ephesians 5:22-24 AMP

46

keep His commandments. We know that we are not under the Law of Moses, but we are still under the Law of Love. If we look at how Jesus demonstrated His love for the church, giving His life for her, we should be willing to give our life in service to Him. If the husband is loving the wife as Christ loved the church, then the wife should be just as willing to serve him.

Submission has become a bad word these days. Everyone is out to get their own needs met and get rid of anyone in their lives who doesn't make them happy. However, the Word of God calls both husbands and wives into submission to each other, out of their reverence and respect for God. This simply means that we should be willing to serve each other. The wife should have no need to exalt her individuality, but rather use her individual abilities to support and help her husband. The wife should be willing to meet the needs of her husband in response to the love he has shown by loving her as Christ loves the church.

As children of God, we are called to love each other even in those times when our spouse is not demonstrating God's love toward us. We must not be selfish because when we make our own needs the top priority, we make it seem as if our spouse's needs are not as important. However, if husbands and wives yield to the love of God, each will be looking to meet the needs of the other and both of their needs will be met.

A wife must understand her husband's need for respect. Let's take a look at the following definition of respect. Respecting your husband means that you notice, regard, esteem, venerate, honor, prefer, defer to, praise, love and admire him.[60] One of the biggest issues for men is a lack of respect. Most women don't know what respect really means to a man. Some might think that it means giving him the biggest portion of food, the best seat, or the Lazy Boy to sit in, but men need to feel like they are admired and have a special place of importance and high

[60]Ephesians 5:33 AMP

regard in their wives' eyes. The wife should be the first to notice how good her husband looks and how hard he works to make her life better. A wife needs to be her husband's number one cheerleader and get behind his dreams. When a man feels like he can do anything, he will.

God has given women the ability to adapt to their surroundings and multi-task. Men are usually not as flexible because they are usually driven by vision and focus. The wife's ability to adapt will help her husband be more flexible when the unexpected happens or when things are out of his control.

CHAPTER 6

MEETING EACH OTHER'S NEEDS

God has placed the husband and wife in the position of caring for and serving one another. We would like to point out two very important things that will help you learn how to meet the needs of your spouse. The first is in I Peter 3:7, which talks about dwelling with one another according to knowledge. The second is in Galatians 5:13, which talks about serving one another in love.

> *"Likewise, ye husbands, dwell with them according to knowledge, giving honour unto the wife, as unto the weaker vessel, and as being heirs together of the grace of life; that your prayers be not hindered."*[61]

DWELLING WITH ONE ANOTHER WITH KNOWLEDGE

Men and women have different needs. These needs must be met in order to have a mutually fulfilled relationship and successful marriage. We must take the time to find out what our spouses' needs are and then with God's help, fulfill those needs. It is important to recognize the difference between a "spiritual" need and a "natural" need. God has not put our spouse in our lives to take His place. Our spouses will never be able to meet our spiritual needs. Many people try to meet their spiritual needs with natural things, but this only leads to frustration and an unfulfilled life. God is our everything—not our spouse.

---

[61] I Peter 3:7 KJV

Don't try to get your spouse to meet your spiritual needs. Jesus told His disciples that He would be with them always, even to the end of the world. Only Jesus could make such a promise. Our spouses cannot make this promise because one day they will die. God never intended for any human being to be all that we need. When God said that it was not good for man to be *alone,* He didn't say that it was not good for man to be *lonely.* God wanted man to experience companionship, just like He created man for companionship with Him. Loneliness results when we become self-focused and not satisfied with what we are doing or who we are.

God does not want us to use fear and manipulation to control our spouse. He doesn't want us to make them feel threatened when we are not pleased with them, or if they for some reason are not able to meet our needs. The Word of God says, *"Be subject to one another out of reverence for Christ (the Messiah, the Anointed One)."*[62] Therefore, there is no room for selfishness. This meeting of each other's needs is to be done willingly, not under fear of being rejected or out of fear that our spouse will leave us. Remember, you did not get married to get something from your spouse. You got married to share what you have to give with your spouse.

THE NEEDS OF THE WIFE

The physical make up of a woman is different than the physical make up of a man. Therefore, there are obviously differences in their need for rest. A woman needs time to renew her emotional and physical well-being. Most women under the age of fifty-five have a cycle each month, yet every woman has a different response to hormonal changes. During pregnancy, a woman may need rest as the baby inside of her demands more nourishment and begins to grow. However, many couples

---

[62]Ephesians 5:21 AMP

continue sexual intimacy during pregnancy. Doctors have affirmed that sexual intimacy can continue during pregnancy up to the point that the woman feels that she is unable to continue, until after the baby is born. That is why I Peter 3:7 says, *"You married men should live considerately with [your wives], with an intelligent recognition [of the marriage relation], honoring the woman as [physically] the weaker, but [realizing that you] are joint heirs of the grace (God's unmerited favor) of life, in order that your prayers may not be hindered and cut off. [Otherwise you cannot pray effectively.]"*[63] " As Pastor Sharon Daugherty has said, "Seek to understand your wife and learn to adjust to her needs."[64]

A woman needs affection (this is not sex!). A woman has more of an emotional and physical need for intimacy. This need can be fulfilled through connecting with her husband through conversation, cuddling, gifts and surprises or through her husband encouraging and building her up around others. When husbands compliment their wives, they are showing verbal appreciation, which is very much needed.

Conversation also shows wives that they are important. It brings them a sense of security and emotional bonding with their husbands. Men are problem solvers so they will naturally want to find a solution when their wives present them with a problem or voice their concerns. However, a woman needs to voice what is in her heart and on her mind. She is not necessarily looking for an answer. She is just seeking comfort and a way to feel connected. Men must have the wisdom to listen, instead of giving an answer or trying to solve the problem.

A woman needs financial security. The husband should be able to support his wife, and if she works, her salary should be for the extras. The Bible says if a man won't work, he shouldn't eat.[65] Remember, in Gen-

---

[63]I Peter 3:7 AMP
[64]Pastor Sharon Daugherty
[65]II Thessalonians 3:10 & I Timothy 5:8 KJV

esis the ground was cursed for man's sake, not for the woman's. The woman was to bear children in pain. Again, we realize that neither the man nor the woman who is a believer is under the curse. However, God always intended for man to take the leadership and responsibility of providing for the woman. When God created Eve, everything had already been done. If a man can't take care of his own needs, he is not ready to get married.

A wife needs her husband to take on the role of a leader, not a dictator. He must be willing to take directions from God, and then in turn give direction and instruction to his family. He must be like Christ and lead by example.

A wife needs her husband to be a dedicated father who spends time with their children. He needs to show affection toward their children—hugging, kissing and playing with them. He also needs to be a disciplinarian and help train them up with a worshipful fear and respect for God.

THE NEEDS OF THE HUSBAND

A wife needs to understand her husband's need for sexual fulfillment. This is a God-given need that must be met. Sex is a form of physical and emotional bonding. Sex helps him think clearly, relax, and focus on what he needs to do emotionally and spiritually. This need is meant to be fulfilled within the marriage relationship and must be tempered by the Spirit of God. The need for sexual fulfillment must not be allowed to cause a man to become undisciplined. It must be balanced with the fruit of self control.

Husbands need recreational companionship. Find something to do together and spend time with each other. He needs an attractive and healthy wife. A woman needs to take care of her body, because taking care of your body is taking care of your spouse. Remember that your body belongs to your spouse.[66]

The husband needs his wife to be supportive and not criticize his decisions for the family. The wife needs to understand his need for admiration and respect. Remember to show verbal appreciation for what your husband does for the family. Don't nag! Always make a thoughtful request, not a selfish demand.

Husbands and wives must have a servant attitude toward each other. You cannot do things the way you did when you were single. You must consider the needs of your spouse. Don't be selfish! You cannot live a single life in a married household. The way you consider one another is by serving one another. During the friendship stage, you took time to get to know your prospective mate. You began to learn what he or she liked. Once you get married, you need to continue to learn what your spouse likes and then do the things that make him or her happy.

(Carl) I remember one day when Charity was running late getting ready for work. I began to look at the time, got upset and criticized her for being late. God spoke to me and convicted me. He told me plainly that she needed help. So I started ironing her clothes and getting our lunch ready to give her more time to get ready. When God gave me this revelation of what it meant to be a servant, it was a turning point in our marriage. As God showed me more things, I began to do more. I began to wash clothes and do things that needed to be done, instead of criticizing or complaining. As a result, there was more peace around the house.

Another revelation that God gave me about the marriage relationship was when He showed me a balancing scale that was moving back and forth. He revealed to me that as long as the scale continues to move, the

---

[66]I Corinthians 7:3-5 KJV

marriage relationship is healthy but once the scale stops, the marriage is in trouble. He revealed to me that a relationship is never 50/50, because one spouse is going to feel like they are doing more than the other spouse. At times, it will feel more like 80/20 or 60/40. The reason why it seems that way is because the partners are serving one another. To think that a relationship will be 50/50 is not scriptural, because this indicates that the underlying motives are based in selfishness. A 50/50 relationship consists of two people who keep a count of what has or has not been done, and whether they feel they are being treated fairly or being cheated. The husband and wife should make it their goal to give 100% to meet the needs of the other and look to God to meet their own needs. *"For you, brethren, have been called to liberty; only do not use liberty as an opportunity for the flesh, but through love serve one another."*[67]

---

[67]Galatians 5:13 NKJV

CHAPTER 7

THE BASICS ON FINANCES

It is important to come into agreement on finances because this is one of the main reasons for divorce. We encourage you to take a finance class with your spouse and learn more. *"Where there is no revelation, the people cast off restraint; but happy is he who keeps the law."*[68]

> *"I appeal to you, brothers, in the name of our Lord Jesus Christ, that all of you agree with one another so that there may be no divisions among you and that you may be perfectly united in mind and thought."*[69]

Husbands and wives must be united concerning their finances. *"Make every effort to keep the unity of the Spirit through the bond of peace."*[70] Find out more about your potential mate's attitude toward money. Their attitude is usually a result of how they were raised and what they have experienced. When you are married, it will no longer be *your* money, but *our* money. Neither should have any secret accounts that the other is not aware of. If one of you is better at keeping account of the finances and managing your checking and savings account, the other should be kept aware of what is being spent and saved. Both of you need to have access to all accounts.

If you have a business, it is important to keep the business finances

[68]Proverbs 29:18 NKJV
[69]I Corinthians 1:10 NIV
[70]Ephesians 4:3 NIV

separate from your personal accounts. Whatever you or your spouse possess, as well as any debts either of you have, will now belong to you both. Go on a shopping trip together and find out how your potential mate spends money. Does he or she just throw things in the basket without looking at the price tag, or does he or she use coupons and comparison shop? Don't go to the grocery store hungry because this usually leads to overspending. You will need to come into agreement on a spending plan, but remember to make room for discretionary funds.

Take time to discuss your views on debt and see if they line up with the Word of God. *"The rich rule over the poor, and the borrower is servant to the lender."*[71] If possible, clean up all debt before the marriage because this will reduce the amount of stress that comes with combining finances.

Find out if your potential mate believes in tithing. *"Bring ye all the tithes into the storehouse, that there may be meat in mine house, and prove me now herewith, saith the LORD of hosts, if I will not open you the windows of heaven, and pour you out a blessing, that there shall not be room enough to receive it."*[72] Both of you should discuss your reasons for tithing or not tithing and find out if you are in agreement. However, the Word of God is clear on this subject, and we believe that tithing causes the blessing of God to come on all you possess—just as the scripture states. *"And here men that die receive tithes; but there he receiveth them, of whom it is witnessed that he liveth."*[73] This scripture lets us know that the principle of tithing did not end with the Old Testament. The blessing of tithing continues today. Tithing began before the written law, when Abraham gave the tithe to Melchizedek in Genesis 14:18-23. Take time to find out whether you are both in agreement and understand this principle of tithing, as well as giving offerings. Don't compromise what you believe

[71]Proverbs 22:7 AMP
[72]Malachi 3:10 KJV
[73]Hebrews 7:8 KJV

the Word of God is saying concerning giving and tithing. Stand firm on this issue, because we believe it will determine whether your finances are blessed, or if you will seem to be putting your money in a bag with holes in it.

Here are some very basic and practical things to think about when setting your spending plan:

1. Life Insurance

2. Medical Insurance

3. Mortgage or Rent

4. Property Taxes

5. Homeowners Insurance

6. Car Payments

7. Car Insurance

8. Electricity

9. Gas

10. Water/Sanitation

11. Telephone

12. Car & Home Maintenance

13. Food Cost

14. Debts

15. Entertainment

16. Clothing

17. Savings and Investments

18. Medical Expenses

19. Miscellaneous

20. Discretionary Funds

Many couples have not considered the importance of having life insurance and medical insurance, but both are necessary and help provide some financial security. You will have a mortgage or rent payment due monthly, unless you are blessed to own property free and clear. When owning a home, you will need to pay property taxes and homeowners insurance. It is also good to consider renters insurance if you're renting. If you are making car payments and your potential mate is making car payments, this will need to be added to the spending plan. Don't forget the utilities, electricity, gas, telephone, water and sanitation. Two people can't eat as cheaply as one. The food cost will nearly double, however if you both work, this should not be a big change. Any debts that either of you hold will now be added to the spending plan. Remember, both of you are responsible to pay these off. Practical things like clothing, entertainment, hair cuts or going to the beauty salon will need to be included. Medical expenses will also need to be considered—annual checkups, occasional medical needs, birth control or other medications. We believe you should put at least 5% or more of your monthly income in a savings account. Also, take a finance class or two and learn about investments. It is also important to have a will or an estate plan with your final wishes clearly stated.

One thing many couples neglect to include in their spending plan is discretionary funds. This is money that both the husband and wife should have to use at their discretion, and yes, this is an allowance. This should be an equal amount for each spouse taken from their weekly, bi-monthly, or monthly income. Having the ability to use a portion of your income at your discretion gives each of you a feeling of freedom to make small purchases and have funds for surprise gifts or outings. This helps each spouse feel better about sticking to a spending plan.

CHAPTER 8

COMMUNICATION GUIDELINES

"Can two walk together, unless they are agreed?"[74]

"Again I say to you that if two of you agree on earth con-cerning anything that they ask, it will be done for them by My Father in heaven. For where two or three are gathered together in My name, I am there in the midst of them."[75]

In this chapter, we want to take the time to explain the power of agree-ment and how important it is to maintain unity in your marriage. The power of agreement begins with effective communication.

During the friendship stage of your relationship, you went through the five levels of communication. It began with the surface level of com-munication. This was when you said "Hello." Maybe you were too shy to say anything else at first, but eventually you moved to the second level of communication and shared the time of day or talked about the weather. Then you moved on to the third level of communication and began to share ideas and opinions. This is where true communication begins. Over time, you have reached the fourth level of communication and expressed feelings and emotions, which is a more personal level of communication. This level of communication requires an atmosphere of acceptance. True friendship begins on this level. Then as your feel-

---

[74]Amos 3:3 NKJV
[75]Matthew 18:19-20 NKJV

ings for each other began to grow, you moved on to the fifth level of communication and began to express your feelings with total openness and honesty. This type of communication must not be lost if the marriage is to grow into maturity.

It is important to be a good listener, not thinking about your response while your spouse is still talking. Good listening also involves good eye contact. Giving your spouse your full attention shows him or her that what they are saying is important to you, and that they are valuable. In the midst of a disagreement, it is important to include reflective listening and repeat what is being said. Much of the misunderstanding in disagreements is caused by prejudging and hearing what we think our spouse has said, but not hearing exactly what was really spoken. We must not project our feelings on what is being said and miss what was really being communicated.

Many of us react to how we feel when disagreements arise, but are not really listening and reacting to what our spouse is saying. When you repeat what you heard, you can make sure the message being communicated is the message being received. Look below the surface of what is being said and ask God to give you an understanding heart.

When things are spoken in anger, there are usually some feelings of hurt and insecurity that have caused those words to be spoken. Deal with the feelings of hurt and insecurity. Don't react to anger. Choose your words carefully and don't speak everything that comes to your mind.[76] When you speak selfish words, you will most likely get a selfish response. Blessing and cursing were not meant to come out of the same mouth.[77] Don't curse your spouse and don't curse at your spouse.[78]

Remember that words are seeds, and seeds were meant to produce

[76]Ephesians 4:31-32; Proverbs 12:18; Proverbs 15:4 Proverbs 21:23 AMP
[77]James 3:10 AMP
[78]James 1:26; Ephesians 4:29-30; Proverbs 4:23-27 AMP

after their own kind, so don't speak anything you don't want to reap back on yourself.[79] For every negative word sown, you will need to sow positive words in their place in order to uproot the negative seed. You have the power to speak life or death to your marriage. [80] *"So then, my beloved brethren, let every man be swift to hear, slow to speak, slow to wrath; for the wrath of man does not produce the righteousness of God."*[81]

When disagreements arise, it is important to be a responder, not a reactor. It takes humility to respond in the right spirit. When you take the time to listen and make sure the message spoken was the message you received, you can respond to what was truly communicated. If you are a reactor, you will most likely react to your own feelings without hearing much of what was communicated. Many families and even countries are at war with each other because of a misunderstanding, or because they reacted to a disagreement. Time was not taken to listen and respond to each other in the right spirit. Dr. Cal Easterling said, "Seek first to understand and then to be understood." We must learn not to take a difference of opinion as a personal attack. It is okay for your mate to have a different opinion than you and this is not unusual, after all, you *are* two different people! You are not in your spouse's life to change him or her to your image, but to learn how their differences can help you grow.

It is important to allow the fruit of the Spirit to operate in your communication with your spouse. Don't allow your feelings to keep you from walking in love and maintaining self-control. *"But the fruit of the Spirit is love, joy, peace, longsuffering, kindness, goodness, faithfulness, gentleness, self-control. Against such there is no law."*[82]

Speak the truth in love according to Ephesians 4:15. Even when you

[79]Genesis 1:11-12; Galatians 6:6-10 KJV
[80]Proverbs 18:21 KJV
[81]James 1:19-20 NKJV
[82]Galatians 5:22-23 NKJV

are expressing an annoyance or irritation, it is important to use words of kindness and respect. If you are too angry to talk in the right spirit, take time to pray and wait until you have calmed down. However, don't let the sun go down upon your wrath.[83] Even if you have to agree to disagree, get the sting of the disagreement out by letting the peace of God rule in your hearts. Don't give the cold shoulder or silent treatment, because this is a form of punishment and a sign of immaturity. We must choose to put an end to strife. Take the word "argument" out of your vocabulary and put the word "disagreement" in its place. An argument is a work of the flesh that brings forth strife, but a disagreement is a difference of opinion and simply needs one Word from God to resolve the situation.

Humble yourself and admit when you've been wrong. Don't grieve the Holy Spirit because of your pride, even when you think you are right. Remember, love gives up the right to be right so we can bring peace and healing to our marriage. This will require dying to self and selfishness.

(Charity) I remember when the Lord spoke to me about being willing to die to self. He simply reminded me what Jesus went through for us. He said that even though He did not require me to get up on a cross and die, I still need to be willing to die to my own way of doing things so the unity in our marriage could grow. At times, it is like childbirth—you go through the stages of growing pains and just when you think you have stretched to your limit, it's time to give birth. The birth speaks of reaching a new level of maturity in your love for your mate. This cannot be born in a selfish relationship in which each of you fight to get your own way. It is only when you have learned to overcome the differences and difficulties of becoming one that you begin to experience true love and fulfillment in your marriage. Love involves giving and sacrificing. This is contrary to what the world believes. The world's way of think-

---

[83]Ephesians 4:26 NKJV

ing is that everyone should stand up for their own rights. They believe that if you're not happy in your marriage, this is reason enough to get a divorce. However, we want to encourage you once again to read I Corinthians the 13th chapter. Renew your mind with the love of God, which is not based on emotions.

Approach all disagreements with a two winner strategy. If one of you feels that you have lost, both of you have lost. If both of you are not able to express your feelings, then neither of you can reach a place of peace and understanding. Stay on one topic at a time and resolve it. Don't bring up a list of things that you disagree on, only deal with the current issue of disagreement. Don't generalize your mate's actions. For example don't say, "You always" or "You never." Own your own feelings and use words like, "I feel" or "That made me feel." It is important not to put your mate in a box and leave him or her no room for change or repentance. When you say things like "You always," this leaves no room for change. This will also put your mate on the defensive, leading to strife instead of a resolution.

Don't bring up the past or use hurtful things that were shared with you in confidence at a moment of vulnerability. Maintain your boundaries. Don't hit below the belt. Don't bring up something that has already been forgiven. Ask your spouse what changes he or she would like you to make, but not in the midst of a disagreement. Work on one issue of change at a time and be led by the Spirit of God. Use the Word of God as your guide and operate in the fruit of the Spirit. Pray for your spouse on a daily basis. Be the initiator of peace and don't wait for your spouse to respond in love first.

CHAPTER 9

GOD'S PLAN FOR THE MARRIAGE BED

"Let marriage be held in honor (esteemed worthy, precious, of great price, and especially dear) in all things. And thus let the marriage bed be undefiled (kept undishonored); for God will judge and punish the unchaste [all guilty of sexual vice] and adulterous."[84]

Undefiled - pure, clean, holy, set apart, to keep your virginity or to maintain the monogamous relationship between you and your spouse.

"Consecrate yourselves therefore, and be holy, for I am the LORD your God."[85]

We realize that these scriptures and the subject of purity in the marriage bed are controversial for many believers. Yet, it is important for us to understand what God's plan for the marriage bed has always been. As we have stated before, God created *one* woman for *one* man. God brought Eve to Adam, blessed them, and told them to be fruitful and multiply. Adam and his wife were both naked, yet they were not ashamed because sin did not exist. God desired for the relationship between husband and wife to be one of unity in every way—spirit, soul and body.

The world would have us only connect in body and soul, neglecting the

[84]Hebrews 13:4 AMP
[85]Leviticus 20:7 NKJV

importance of spiritual oneness. When you have sex with someone outside of marriage, there is no spiritual unity or commitment. However, because sex involves all three parts of your being, you form a soul tie that is not easily broken. When this soul tie is created, it forms a permanent impression on your conscience that only God's supernatural grace and power can remove. Everyone who has ever engaged in a consenting sexual relationship understands that there is a craving that is created for continued sexual relations. This is God's design for sex, but He intended it to only be experienced in the confines of marriage. The bond that forms from sexual intimacy was never intended to be broken or shared with multiple partners.

There is a physical exchange between sexual partners. This is why we see such an uncontrolled outbreak of sexually transmitted diseases. The world has fallen into the philosophy that sex is just a physical expression and should be done without restraint. However, the lack of sexual restraint has never been freeing, but rather causes everyone who gives in to it to become a slave to sexual vice. This does not mean that everyone who has ever engaged in sex outside of marriage has no self-control, but once the door to sexual sin has been opened, it can only be shut by dying to the flesh. *"Therefore put to death your members which are on the earth: fornication, uncleanness, passion, evil desire, and covetousness, which is idolatry. Because of these things the wrath of God is coming upon the sons of disobedience, in which you yourselves once walked when you lived in them."*[86] Dying to self or selfishness is a process every Christian who chooses to live according to the Word of God must do. It takes much more time and effort to put to death something that has a strong grip on you than to maintain control over your body.

The Bible states that sexual sin is unlike other forms of sin because you sin against your own body. *"Flee fornication. Every sin that a man doeth*

---

[86]Colossians 3:5-7 NKJV

is without the body; but he that committeth fornication sinneth against his own body."[87]   The body has a memory that has now been formed, and a craving has begun that was designed to be fulfilled in marriage. When this craving is created outside of the bond of marriage, it may result in a lack of self control, making it hard to be satisfied with sex within a monogamous marriage union.

Like any other habit that is created, this can also be overcome. However, we cannot use sheer will power. We need the Spirit of God and the Word of God to bring our flesh back under subjection to the will of God. We are now fighting a battle against the desires of our flesh that are in direct opposition to the will of God.

Many people believe that because God is forgiving, we don't have to do everything the Word of God says. This ignores the reason God put these boundaries in place. These boundaries were put in place to protect us from the results of sin and bondage of being controlled by our flesh. For instance, we give our children boundaries by telling them to look both ways before crossing the street or by telling them not to play with fire. Likewise, God has given us boundaries through His Word for our protection.

Let's examine some additional reasons why sex was intended for marriage. Remember, sex is a sign of covenant—keeping yourself only for each other for as long as you both shall live. This may sound unbelievable in this day and age, but it is still God's plan. When we choose His plan, we receive His blessing. God designed sex for procreation, to be a part of the cleaving between husband and wife, for mutual pleasure, to be an expression of affection, and for emotional and intellectual bonding. Sex was meant to bring husbands and wives to a deeper level of intimacy. This is not to be taken lightly or as a casual expression of a physical urge. Sex is so much more than that. However, when we agree

[87] I Corinthians 6:18 KJV

with the world's philosophy on sex, we choose the cheaper in place of the deeper. This usually results in short term unfulfilling relationships. When we choose God's plan for sex and keep ourselves pure for the marriage bed, even if we have sinned in the past, God will restore what was lost. The most fulfilling relationships are the ones we have grown and developed in when we loved someone according to the Word, not our feelings.

God designed our bodies. He is not against the enjoyment of sexual relations between a husband and wife. *"You have stolen my heart, my sister, my bride; you have stolen my heart with one glance of your eyes, with one jewel of your necklace. How delightful is your love, my sister, my bride! How much more pleasing is your love than wine, and the fragrance of your perfume than any spice! Awake, north wind, and come, south wind! Blow on my garden, that its fragrance may spread abroad. Let my lover come into his garden and taste its choice fruits."*[88] In this passage of scripture, there is an expression of a strong desire for sexual relations between a husband and wife. The marriage bed is to be enjoyed by married couples, yet boundaries must still be maintained. It's important not to allow things like pornography and lust to pollute the marriage bed. That's why even the sexual relations between husband and wife should be protected. Pastor Sharon Daugherty said, "Praying together regularly helps guard your heart and soul." Sexual unity between a husband and wife is an outward sign of an inward bond. It is a time of concentrating on each other and shutting everyone else out.

Men need the patience and knowledge to make sure their wives have a pleasurable sexual experience. There is no room for selfishness, because this is meant to be a time of mutual pleasure and meeting of each other's needs. It is important to maintain frequency and consistency in sexual relations between a husband and wife. *"The husband should ful-*

[88]Song of Solomon 4:9-10,16 AMP

fill his marital duty to his wife, and likewise the wife to her husband. The wife's body does not belong to her alone but also to her husband. In the same way, the husband's body does not belong to him alone but also to his wife. Do not deprive each other except by mutual consent and for a time, so that you may devote yourselves to prayer. Then come together again so that Satan will not tempt you because of your lack of self-control."[89] We must be willing to fulfill our spouse's need for sexual fulfillment. This need may be greater in the husband, but it is a God- given need and should be a natural expression of affection. Husbands also need their wives to initiate sexual intimacy. Remember, you belong to each other and your bodies are not your own. Do not deprive each other of sexual unity, and do not use sex as a tool to control your spouse. Be willing to meet each other's need for sexual unity. Make the time of sexual intimacy a priority in your marriage. Maintain your privacy, keep your sexual relations with your spouse between the two of you. Don't discuss this with friends or family. Pastor Sharon Daugherty advises, "The only time you should discuss your sexual relations with someone else is when you are seeking counsel." If you go to a counselor, only discuss what you and your spouse agree that the counselor should know about your sexual relations.

There are various things that attempt to rob husbands and wives from experiencing a blessed and fulfilling marriage bed. Some of these are:

- Bad experiences in the past, including sexual abuse or premarital sex.

- Vain imaginations caused by impure thoughts, which were introduced through pornography, movies, television, or other avenues.[90]

---

[89]I Corinthians 7:3-5 AMP
[90]II Corinthians 10; Hebrews 13:4 KJV

- Lack of desire caused by unforgiveness, anger, bitterness, tiredness, etc....[91]

- Not understanding the difference between men and women and their arousals.[92]

- Selfishness, which can lead to a lack of desire if both spouses' sexual needs are not being met.

- Fear of becoming pregnant can cause a lack of desire, but you need to come into agreement on whether you will use birth control and what form is best for both of you.

- Weariness from responsibilities such as work and children.

- Distractions such as the phone, TV or internet.

When you make a decision to work at your marital relationship, you seek to recognize these situations and if they exist, you resolve to overcome them.[93] If there are areas in your life that still need to be healed, remember God wants us to be healed from our past and to walk in unconditional love toward our spouse. Make a commitment to God to walk in understanding and in the fruit of the Spirit in your relationship with your spouse.

[91]Genesis 3:16; Philippians 2:3-4; Psalm 34:14 KJV
[92]I Peter 3:7 KJV
[93]Pastor Sharon Daugherty

CHAPTER 10

BUILDING HEDGES AROUND YOUR MARRIAGE

"Have You not put a hedge about him and his house and all that he has, on every side? You have conferred prosperity and happiness upon him in the work of his hands, and his possessions have increased in the land."[94]

A **hedge** or **hedgerow** is a line of closely spaced shrubs and tree species, planted and trained in such a way as to form a barrier or to mark the boundary of an area. Hedges used to separate a road from adjoining fields or one field from another, and of sufficient age to incorporate larger trees, are known as hedgerows."

There are several hedges that need to be built around your marriage to protect it from wrong influences and outside forces. The first hedge that should be built in your marriage is unconditional love. The second hedge to be built in your marriage is prayer and confessing God's Word over your spouse. The third hedge is trusting that your spouse knows the voice of God. The fourth hedge is being led by the Spirit of God. The fifth hedge to be built in your marriage is honoring your spouse as a child of God. These hedges are given in no particular order, but the love of God is always the place to start. You should be building on each of these hedges throughout your marriage.

---

[94]Job 1:10 - AMP

HEDGE #1: UNCONDITIONAL LOVE

As we have mentioned in previous chapters, I Corinthians the 13th chapter is the pattern for walking in unconditional love, especially with your spouse. Love gives of itself without expecting anything in return. Many times in marriage, it may seem like your spouse is not loving you unconditionally, but this is no excuse to be unforgiving or to withdraw from loving them. Unless you walk in unconditional love, your love will never grow or develop the way God intended it to. *"I assure you, most solemnly I tell you, unless a grain of wheat falls into the earth and dies, it remains [just one grain; it never becomes more but lives] by itself alone. But if it dies, it produces many others and yields a rich harvest."*[95] Love grows in times of adversity and increases when you choose to work through differences and decide not to quit.

When love is tested, it manifests the fruit of the Spirit, but when selfishness is tested, it manifests the works of the flesh. *"And we have known and believed the love that God has for us. God is love, and he who abides in love abides in God, and God in him."*[96] God wants us to follow His example of love, not give in to our emotions. If you are led by your emotions, you will always be unstable because your emotions change based on the situation in which you find yourself. Love is not based on emotions; it is a choice that must be made continually regardless of the circumstances you face.

It takes time to adapt to the differences in each other's personalities. You will have to make adjustments as you grow into oneness with your spouse. Unconditional love gives you the grace and flexibility to make the necessary adjustments to accommodate these differences. As a result of your willingness to adjust to the needs and differences in your spouse, you will grow and mature in ways you would not if you were to

[95]John 12:24 AMP
[96]I John 4:16 NKJV

74

give in to selfishness. Your relationship grows everyday as you submit to one another and allow God to give you an answer to every roadblock you face in your relationship. Remember, you are not just giving in to your spouse, you are submitting to God. It is not about who will have the last word but rather giving God's Word priority while both of you submit to His will.

There is no weapon that is formed against you that shall prosper when you are walking in the unconditional love of God. This especially applies to the unconditional love that you are required to walk in toward your spouse. As a couple, you will need to stay in the Word and in prayer in order to maintain unity and be led by the Spirit of God instead of your flesh.

HEDGE #2: *PRAYER & CONFESSING GOD'S WORD OVER YOUR SPOUSE*

"Husbands, love your wives, just as Christ also loved the church and gave Himself for her, that He might sanctify and cleanse her with the washing of water by the word, that He might present her to Himself a glorious church, not having spot or wrinkle or any such thing, but that she should be holy and without blemish."[97]

Remember, you will have what you say. That's why it is so important to speak what God's Word says over your spouse (Mark 11:23-25). Don't allow your negative feelings to control what you say about your spouse. It is during those times of disagreement that you need to put God's Word in your mouth and confess what it says, even if your spouse is not acting in line with that word.

Be willing to walk in forgiveness, even if your spouse doesn't ask to be forgiven. Sometimes what you perceive to be wrong does not seem

---

[97]Ephesians 5:25-27 - NKJV

wrong to your spouse. This could be due to selfishness, but it is also due to a difference in the way you think about things. It is also due to the differences in your experiences, how you were raised or other factors. That is why it is so important not to be quick to get angry or offended. With time you will learn each other's ways and know how to communicate more effectively. You will come to a better understanding of how to treat one another.

It is so important to get to know each other by the spirit first then you can trust the heart of the person, even when there is a difference of opinion. *"The LORD'S LIGHT PENETRATES THE HUMAN SPIRIT, EXPOSING EVERY HIDDEN MOTIVE."* *"The spirit of man [that factor in human personality which proceeds immediately from God] is the lamp of the Lord, searching all his innermost parts."*[98] This scripture tells us that it is the spirit, or the heart of man, that God searches. The heart reveals our true motives.

In order to know each other by the Spirit, you must take time to pray in the Spirit together. The Bible tells us in Romans 8:26-28 that the Spirit makes intercession for us according to the will of God. Since the Spirit of God knows the mind of God, He is able to pray for us according to God's will. He can also reveal the will of God to us. We need the ministry of the Holy Spirit operating in our marriage to bring us to a place of understanding the will of God, as well as our mate. The Holy Spirit helps us see each other through God's eyes. The Spirit of God reveals the truth to us and brings us to a place of submission to God's will over our own will. He causes us to submit to one another in the fear of God, or out of reverence for God. God brings us into balance with one another and reveals to us whether we need to die to our flesh or resist the attack of the enemy.

---

[98]Proverbs 20:38 NLT & AMP

HEDGE #3: *TRUSTING THAT YOUR SPOUSE KNOWS THE VOICE OF GOD*

"The sheep that are My own hear and are listening to My voice; and I know them, and they follow Me."[99]

During the friendship stage of your relationship, it is important to take the time to pray together. Get to know how God speaks to your potential mate. Get to know each other by the spirit. This will build your confidence in your mate's ability to hear from God. While we were in the friendship stages of our relationship, we took time to pray and read the Word each time we got together. This continued during our engagement. We started out talking about what we believed God wanted us to do in the future, as well as the present. We spent time talking about God's Word and enjoying spiritual things such as gospel music, visiting churches and singing in the choir. Our love for God seemed to draw us closer to each other, and it continues to do so today.

(Carl) I remember when God told me that our time was up in New York and that we were entering into a new season in our life and ministry. I spoke to Charity and asked her if God had spoken to her about leaving New York, but she said *no*. I trusted that she knew the voice of God so I put that aside and let God speak to her in His own way. I knew that Charity was very attached to her family so if I had tried to force her to leave, it would have caused more division in our marriage. It also would have led her to question whether God had spoken to me.

Two years later, God gave her a dream that showed her what was holding her back from trusting God's will for us to leave. I came home from work one day and Charity had boxes packed—blocking the doorway. God had spoken to her so she did not need to be talked into or convinced to leave New York. She knew it was the will of God. It is so important to

---

[99]John 10:27 - AMP

allow your spouse to hear from God for themselves, so there will be no room for doubt or for the enemy to bring division into your marriage. If God has spoken it, He will confirm it, and it will stand the test of time. By allowing her time to hear from God without being pressured or coerced by me, it gave her confidence that it was God's will, not just mine. No one wants to be controlled by someone else. We should give our spouse the same freedom to hear God's voice that we desire. If you don't trust that your potential mate knows the voice of God, you should not marry them. *"Can two walk together, except they be agreed?"*[100]

(Charity) When Carl asked if I had heard from the Lord about leaving New York, I can honestly say I hadn't. I was so involved in our church and comfortable with my dad's leadership as pastor. For two years, Carl never asked me if I had heard from God yet. Then two years later I had a dream and in that dream, God showed me what was holding me back. I saw a small fish under the control of a bigger fish. The small fish followed the bigger fish and did whatever the bigger fish did. The smaller fish finally jumped out of the water and was flopping around on land. When I woke up, the Lord spoke to my spirit and explained that I was the smaller fish. I was afraid to leave the bigger fish (my dad), because I was more comfortable being under his authority and trusted his spiritual leadership more than I trusted God and the leadership of my husband. This really opened my eyes and made me realize that if I didn't leave at this point, I would be operating in fear. As an act of my faith, I began packing boxes not even knowing where we were going. I knew it was time to leave. Now, Carl and I could come into agreement and believe God for direction and the finances to leave.

We spoke to my parents, and my mom felt that she heard from God about connecting us with a pastor we knew in Tulsa. He was a minister friend who had previously lived in New Jersey and was part of a fellow-

---

[100]Amos 3:3 KJV

ship of churches with which my dad was affiliated. Carl prayed about it first and felt that we should contact the pastor. When we did, he said that he had received a prophetic word telling him that someone from his old stomping grounds would be coming to help him. We came to Tulsa and began looking for a place to live and were led to a relocation company. The agent working with us was a believer and was able to get Carl a job without an interview. He took us to an apartment complex and they approved us with our previous rental history and a letter from the employer of the company that hired Carl without even meeting him first. We got the apartment and returned to New York to finish getting everything ready to leave. We didn't even have all of the funds we needed to move. Two days before we were supposed to leave, our church decided to have a special service for us. They took up an offering for us and it was just what we needed to pay for the moving trailer and all of our moving expenses. Praise God!

"And let the peace (soul harmony which comes) from Christ rule (act as umpire continually) in your hearts [deciding and settling with finality all questions that arise in your minds, in that peaceful state] to which as [members of Christ's] one body you were also called [to live]. And be thankful (appreciative), [giving praise to God always]."[101]

HEDGE #4: *BEING LED BY THE SPIRIT OF GOD*

"For as many as are led by the Spirit of God, they are the sons of God."[102]

We need to continue to rely on the ministry of the Holy Spirit as a couple. The Holy Spirit's job is to bring us into oneness with God. When we are both one with God, we will be one with each other, just as Jesus prayed *"that they all may be one, as You, Father, are in Me, and I in You;*

---

[101]Colossians 3:15 AMP
[102]Romans 8:14 - KJV

that they also may be one in Us, that the world may believe that You sent Me. And the glory which You gave Me I have given them, that they may be one just as We are one: I in them, and You in Me; that they may be made perfect in one, and that the world may know that You have sent Me, and have loved them as You have loved Me."[103] This is what submitting to one another in the fear of God means.

During our times of prayer at home, God directed us to begin to flow in the gifts of the Spirit together. This began to build Charity's confidence in speaking out what the Spirit of God was saying to her. There was no pressure to be accurate, even though the goal was to speak exactly what the Holy Spirit was saying. We judged the things that were said by the Word of God, because the Spirit and the Word agree. We both felt free to flow in the gifts of the Spirit together. As we began to develop in hearing from God in prayer together, many times Charity would give a word in tongues and I would give the interpretation in English. We each began to hear different parts of what God was saying to us as a couple, receiving His instruction together. God was developing our ministry as a couple, and still continues to do so. This doesn't mean that we will always minister together as a couple, but our ministry is one.

HEDGE #5: *HONORING YOUR SPOUSE AS A CHILD OF GOD*

"For he who eats and drinks in an unworthy manner eats and drinks judgment to himself, not discerning the Lord's body. For this reason many are weak and sick among you, and many sleep."[104]

Husbands and wives must remember that their spouse is a member of the body of Christ and that the Spirit of God dwells in them. Honoring your spouse as a child of God is rightly discerning the body of Christ. Many Christian husbands forget that their spouse is a member of the

---

[103]John 17:21-23 NKJV
[104]I Corinthians 11:29-30 -NKJV

body of Christ, so they begin to abuse them. This is why their prayers are hindered and some die an early death. This can also cause many trials and tribulations to come into their lives.

Ephesians 5:21-31 tells us how husbands and wives should treat each other. It uses Christ and the church as the example. If we follow the pattern given in this scripture, we will have the kind of results we desire in our marriage. When a husband treats his wife like Christ treated the church, by laying down his life for her (wife), his wife will respond by submitting to him just like the church is called to submit to Christ. Both are called to submit to each other out of reverence for God, honoring God's commandment of love. This means that the husband will not take advantage of his wife as the weaker vessel. It also means that the wife will not take advantage of her husband through selfishness.

It is our desire that those in leadership in the church who are married would set the example of honoring their spouse for the younger couples in their ministry. This should be evidenced by the way they treat their spouse in public, as well as in private. They need to regularly express how important their spouse is to their life and ministry. They should not be in competition with each other, but rather prefer their spouse over themselves. Remember, if you have strong families in your church, you will have a strong church, and it starts with you.

"Let deacons be the husbands of one wife, ruling their children and their own houses well."[105]

---

[105] I Timothy 3:12 NKJV

CHAPTER 11

BLENDING FAMILIES

"Finally, all [of you] should be of one and the same mind (united in spirit), sympathizing [with one another], loving [each other] as brethren [of one household], compassionate and courteous (tenderhearted and humble)."[106]

Blending families involves blending different family backgrounds, including financial differences, cultural differences, and blending divorced families. It is important to make the choice not to focus on the differences, but to be led by the Spirit of God.

When a couple is dealing with children from a previous marriage, there is definitely a different set of challenges in blending their families. However, when dealing with divorced families, it is important to have patience and allow time for adjustment. When a single parent who has children from his or her previous marriage begins to introduce a potential mate to his or her children, it is important to take it slow. Take time to develop your friendship and include your children.

Children need consistency. They are possibly dealing with feelings of abandonment, insecurity, and rejection. Make sure that you address the feelings your children are dealing with prior to beginning a new relationship. If your children are having a hard time talking about some of their feelings, don't ignore them. Get counseling if you are unable

---

[106]I Peter 3: 8 -AMP

to speak to your children about what they feel. Many times we don't allow enough time for ourselves or our loved ones to heal or deal with the emotions that divorce causes in our lives. When these feelings are not dealt with and the divorced family does not confront the issue that led to the breakup of the previous marriage, it will carry over into the new marriage. Children will possibly begin to resent the new mate and their parent, because they wanted their biological parents to get back together. This should have been discussed earlier. Even if the children still want their parents to be reunited, their parents should discuss why this will not happen. Make sure your children know that it's not their fault that the divorce happened. Be willing to ask your children for forgiveness for the breakup of their family. Do your best to explain what you believe went wrong. Don't be too detailed, but make sure to address the core reason for the divorce. Let your children talk about how the divorce makes them feel then validate their feelings with words of acceptance and love.

Whether you have lost your mate through death or divorce, time is needed to deal with the emotions of grief, anger, regret, sadness, resentment and failure. Take time to acknowledge these feelings and bring them before God in prayer. Seek godly counsel from other Christians who have experienced this same kind of loss. Spend time allowing the ministry of the Holy Spirit to bring comfort to you through His Word.

The following tells us that Jesus has come to take away our grief and replace it with the knowledge of His unconditional love. *"The Spirit of the Lord GOD is upon Me, because the LORD has anointed Me to preach good tidings to the poor; He has sent Me to heal the brokenhearted, to proclaim liberty to the captives, and the opening of the prison to those who are bound; to proclaim the acceptable year of the LORD, and the day of vengeance of our God; to comfort all who mourn, to console those who mourn in Zion, to give them beauty for ashes, the oil of joy for mourning, the gar-*

ment of praise for the spirit of heaviness; that they may be called trees of righteousness, the planting of the LORD, that He may be glorified."[107]

Make sure you maintain proper boundaries in your new relationship and don't bring your potential mate into your home overnight. Remember, you are still to live a Christ-like life in front of your children, even after you have made mistakes in the past. *"What shall we say then? Shall we continue in sin, that grace may abound? God forbid. How shall we, that are dead to sin, live any longer therein?"*[108] Sex before marriage is fornication. Sex with someone other than your spouse, when you are married, is adultery. God's Word doesn't change to fit our circumstances, we have to change our way of doing things to live according to God's Word. We believe that sex before marriage is one of the reasons so many couples get divorced. These couples let their fleshly desires start the relationship, therefore since they are used to giving in to the flesh, they lack the will to die to selfishness and the marriage ends in divorce.

Some think of divorced families as the only families that have to be blended, but we believe that when two different people get married there is a lot of blending of differences that must take place. We already talked about how our mate will have a different way of thinking. This is partly due to the way they were raised and their life experiences. This shapes the way we think, the priorities we set, and the things we do. However, as a believer we are to set our standards based on the Word of God instead of on our background or experiences. God's Word tells us to know no man after the flesh.[109] This means that we are to know each other based on more than just physical appearance or emotion. It takes time to get to know someone, especially when you are not focusing on the outward appearance. Take time to get to know your potential mate—get to know their history, what makes them who

---

[107]Isaiah 61:1-3 NKJV
[108]Romans 6:1-2 KJV
[109]II Corinthians 5:14-17 KJV

they are, and examine what makes them so attractive to you. Go beyond the surface and ask the Holy Spirit to show you whether they are compatible to you.

Your different family backgrounds will also play a major role in how well you blend your new family. Many people think that their mate will now become a part of their family or be adopted as a member of their existing family. However, you and your new mate will start a new family that didn't previously exist, so they do not just become a part of your existing family. It is important to set up a standard for your new household to see yourself as part of this new family. Just like the wife normally takes on the last name of her husband, a new address, and a marriage license with Mr. and Mrs. (last name), this shows that a new family has just begun. This should be seen as a new beginning with a fresh start. It should be based on God's standards, not the traditions, mistakes, or failures of your previous family relationships. The standard of the Word of God is ultimately our goal in raising our new family. God's standard is based on unconditional love.

We have previously mentioned that it is important to seek your parents' approval when choosing a mate, but we realize that some will need to seek the advice of spiritual counselors if they don't have a relationship with parents who love them. Some of the difficulties we have seen are the result of parents basing their decision for not accepting their child's choice of a mate on things that are not spiritual, such as cultural or ethnic differences. If the difference is not based on Godly standards, such as being unequally yoked to an unbeliever, then the decision to marry or not to marry should be made based on true spiritual incompatibility or issues of lack of wholeness in the life of the potential mate. Please remember that we all descended from Adam and Eve, so there is only one race of people on the earth, and that is the human race. However, since the tower of Babel, many different ethnic groups or nationalities exist, but this is not a reason to consider a person to be incompatible. If you have taken the time to develop your friendship, as we mentioned in the chapter on compatibility, all the questions of incompatibility should be answered before you consider someone as a potential mate. None of these questions of incompatibility should be based on ethnic differences. However, remember that your culture should not take precedence over the Word of God. If your culture teaches you to do something against the Word of God, then you should obey God, not your culture.

Blending families with different cultural backgrounds should be a good experience, not something to be feared. All ethnic groups will share the same heaven. We believe God is pleased when we learn how to love all His people, regardless of their ethnic differences.

> *"Do not lie to one another, for you have stripped off the old (unregenerate) self with its evil practices, and have clothed yourselves with the new [spiritual self], which is [ever in the process of being] renewed and remolded into [fuller and more perfect knowledge upon] knowledge after the image (the likeness) of Him Who created it. [In this new creation all distinctions vanish.] There is no room for and there can be neither Greek nor Jew, circumcised nor uncircumcised, [nor difference between nations whether alien] barbarians or Scythians [who are the most savage of all], nor slave or free man; but Christ is all and in all [everything and everywhere, to all men, without distinction of person]. Clothe yourselves therefore, as God's own chosen ones (His own picked representatives), [who are] purified and holy and well-beloved [by God Himself, by putting on behavior marked by] tenderhearted pity and mercy, kind feeling, a lowly opinion of yourselves, gentle ways, [and] patience [which is tireless and long-suffering, and has the*

power to endure whatever comes, with good temper]."[110]

Let the Word of God have the final authority over your choice for a mate, and ultimately over your marriage.

---

[110]Colossians 3:9-12 AMP

PRACTICAL APPLICATION MANUAL

CHAPTER 1 - *PRACTICAL APPLICATION*

WHOLENESS

In this chapter, we discussed what it means to be whole, and how important it is to achieve wholeness before entering into marriage.

"But let patience have its perfect work, that you may be perfect and complete, lacking nothing."[111]

I. DISCOVERING THE HOLES - JOHN 5:2-9; REVELATION 7:17; 21:4

Take a look at yourself and see if you are complete within yourself. Ask yourself the following questions.

    A. Are you haunted by memories of past failures and/or abuse? (If so, list them)

_____

_____

_____

_____

_____

    B. Have you been hurt by family, friends or past relationships? (Write down the names)

_____

_____

[111]James 1:4 NKJV

_____

_____

_____

C. Were you physically or emotionally abused? (Write down the names & what the abuse was)

_____

_____

_____

_____

_____

D. Have you experienced the death of a spouse? Divorce? How long has it been?

_____

_____

_____

_____

_____

II. THE HEALING PROCESS - EPHESIANS 3:17-19

[17]"That Christ may dwell in your hearts through faith; that you, being rooted and grounded in love, may be able to comprehend with all the saints what is the width and length and depth and height— to know the love of Christ which passes knowledge; that you may be filled with all the fullness of God" (NKJV).

A. Understanding the love of God - I Corinthians 13th Chapter; Romans 5:8; 8:35-39

   1. Have you taken time to build a strong relationship with God? How much time do you devote daily to prayer and meditating on the Word of God?

   _____

   _____

   _____

   _____

   _____

   2. Have you allowed the love of God to uproot any feelings of hurt and/or unforgiveness? What have you done to release these feelings?

   _____

   _____

   _____

   _____

   _____

   3. Do you have an understanding of God's unconditional love for you? (Please explain what this unconditional love means to you.)

   _____

   _____

   _____

   _____

   _____

4. Have you forgiven the person(s) who hurt or abused you?
   (List the names.) How long ago?

   _____

   _____

   _____

   _____

   _____

5. Have you allowed God to give you a love for the person(s)
   who hurt or abused you? Do you pray for them? (If so, list
   the names.)

   _____

   _____

   _____

   _____

   _____

6. If you have abused anyone, have you stopped the abuse?
   Have you asked that person(s) for forgiveness? (If so, the list
   names.) _____

   _____

   _____

   _____

   _____

B. Finding out who you are and what you have in Christ - I Corinthians 1:30-31;

II Corinthians 5:21; Romans 8:14-17; 5:17-21; Ephesians chapters 1-3

1.   Take time to meditate on scriptures that tell you who you are and what you have in Christ. Create a list of scriptures for daily confession like the ones listed above. Put your name in the scripture to personalize it.

     (i.e. - According as He has chosen (insert your name) in Him before the foundation of the world that (insert your name) should be holy and without blame before him in love."[112])

_____

_____

_____

_____

_____

_____

_____

_____

_____

_____

_____

_____

_____

_____

_____

_____

_____

[112]Ephesians 1:4 KJV

_____

_____

_____

_____

_____

_____

_____

_____

_____

_____

_____

_____

C. Learn the importance of yielding to the ministry of the Holy Spirit

1. *"So too the [Holy] Spirit comes to our aid and bears us up in our weakness; for we do not know what prayer to offer nor how to offer it worthily as we ought, but the Spirit Himself goes to meet our supplication and pleads in our behalf with unspeakable yearnings and groanings too deep for utterance."*[113]

Do you spend time praying in the spirit (praying in other tongues) on a daily basis? If so, how has this helped you?

_____

_____

_____

[113] Romans 8:26 AMP

2. "But the Comforter (Counselor, Helper, Intercessor, Advocate, Strengthener, Standby), the Holy Spirit, Whom the Father will send in My name [in My place, to represent Me and act on My behalf], He will teach you all things. And He will cause you to recall (will remind you of, bring to your remembrance) everything I have told you."[114]

Have you experienced the comfort, counsel, help, intercession, strength and all around ministry of the Holy Spirit in your life? What has this done for you?

_____

_____

_____

_____

_____

3. "However, I am telling you nothing but the truth when I say it is profitable (good, expedient, advantageous) for you that I go away. Because if I do not go away, the Comforter (Counselor, Helper, Advocate, Intercessor, Strengthener, Standby) will not come to you [into close fellowship with you]; but if I go away, I will send Him to you [to be in close fellowship with you]. And when He comes, He will convict and convince the world and bring demonstration to it about sin and about righteousness (uprightness of heart and right standing with God) and about judgment:"[115]

Have you noticed a change in your heart and your way of thinking as a result of spending time reading the Word of God and praying in the spirit? List the changes you have

[114]St. John 14:26 AMP
[115]John 16:7-8 AMP

seen.

_____
_____
_____
_____
_____

4."But when He, the Spirit of Truth (the Truth-giving Spirit) comes, He will guide you into all the Truth (the whole, full Truth). For He will not speak His own message [on His own authority]; but He will tell whatever He hears [from the Father; He will give the message that has been given to Him], and He will announce and declare to you the things that are to come [that will happen in the future]. He will honor and glorify Me, because He will take of (receive, draw upon) what is Mine and will reveal (declare, disclose, transmit) it to you."116

Has the Holy Spirit revealed to you God's plans and purposes for your future? (Please explain)

_____
_____
_____
_____
_____
_____
_____
_____
_____

116John 16:13-14 AMP

III. ACHIEVING WHOLENESS

"Then Jesus said to those Jews who believed Him, 'If you abide in My word, you are My disciples indeed. And you shall know the truth, and the truth shall make you free.'[117]

A. Allow patience to produce in you wholeness through your tests and hardships.

"Consider it wholly joyful, my brethren, whenever you are enveloped in or encounter trials of any sort or fall into various temptations. Be assured and understand that the trial and proving of your faith bring out endurance and steadfastness and patience. But let endurance and steadfastness and patience have full play and do a thorough work, so that you may be [people] perfectly and fully developed [with no defects], lacking in nothing."[118]

B. Equip yourself to overcome the attacks of the enemy with the Word of God.

" In conclusion, be strong in the Lord [be empowered through your union with Him]; draw your strength from Him [that strength which His boundless might provides]. Put on God's whole armor [the armor of a heavy-armed soldier which God supplies], that you may be able successfully to stand up against [all] the strategies and the deceits of the devil. For we are not wrestling with flesh and blood [contending only with physical opponents], but against the despotisms, against the powers, against [the master spirits who are] the world rulers of this present darkness, against the spirit forces of wickedness in the heavenly (supernatural) sphere. Therefore put on God's complete armor, that you may be able to resist and stand your ground on the evil day [of danger], and, having done all [the crisis demands], to stand [firmly in your place]. Stand therefore

[117]John 8:31-32 NKJV
[118]James 1:2-4 AMP

[hold your ground], having tightened the belt of truth around your loins and having put on the breastplate of integrity and of moral rectitude and right standing with God, and having shod your feet in preparation [to face the enemy with the firm-footed stability, the promptness, and the readiness produced by the good news] of the Gospel of peace. Lift up over all the [covering] shield of saving faith, upon which you can quench all the flaming missiles of the wicked [one]. And take the helmet of salvation and the sword that the Spirit wields, which is the Word of God. Pray at all times (on every occasion, in every season) in the Spirit, with all [manner of] prayer and entreaty. To that end keep alert and watch with strong purpose and perseverance, interceding in behalf of all the saints (God's consecrated people)." [119]

C. Renew your mind with the Word of God.

"Do not be conformed to this world (this age), [fashioned after and adapted to its external, superficial customs], but be transformed (changed) by the [entire] renewal of your mind [by its new ideals and its new attitude], so that you may prove [for yourselves] what is the good and acceptable and perfect will of God, even the thing which is good and acceptable and perfect [in His sight for you]." [120]

"For though we walk (live) in the flesh, we are not carrying on our warfare according to the flesh and using mere human weapons. For the weapons of our warfare are not physical [weapons of flesh and blood], but they are mighty before God for the overthrow and destruction of strongholds, [inasmuch as we] refute arguments and theories and reasonings and every proud and lofty thing that sets itself up against the [true] knowledge of God; and we lead every thought and purpose away captive into the obedience of Christ (the Messiah, the Anointed One), being in readiness to punish every [in-

---

[119]Ephesians 6:10-18 AMP
[120]Romans 12:2 AMP

subordinate for his] disobedience, when your own submission and obedience [as a church] are fully secured and complete." [121]

D. Build yourself up by praying in the Holy Spirit.

"But you, beloved, build yourselves up [founded] on your most holy faith [make progress, rise like an edifice higher and higher], praying in the Holy Spirit; Guard and keep yourselves in the love of God; expect and patiently wait for the mercy of our Lord Jesus Christ (the Messiah)—[which will bring you] unto life eternal." [122]

1. Humble yourself before God.

"Humble yourselves therefore under the mighty hand of God, that he may exalt you in due time." [123]

"So be subject to God. Resist the devil [stand firm against him], and he will flee from you. Come close to God and He will come close to you. [Recognize that you are] sinners, get your soiled hands clean; [realize that you have been disloyal] wavering individuals with divided interests, and purify your hearts [of your spiritual adultery]. [As you draw near to God] be deeply penitent and grieve, even weep [over your disloyalty]. Let your laughter be turned to grief and your mirth to dejection and heartfelt shame [for your sins]. Humble yourselves [feeling very insignificant] in the presence of the Lord, and He will exalt you [He will lift you up and make your lives significant]." [124]

2. Stand fast in your liberty.

"In [this] freedom Christ has made us free [and completely liberated us]; stand fast then, and do not be hampered and held en-

[121]II Corinthians 10:3-6 AMP
[122]Jude 1:20-21 AMP
[123]I Peter 5:6 KJV
[124]James 4:7-10 AMP

snared and submit again to a yoke of slavery [which you have once put off]."[125]

CHAPTER 2 - PRACTICAL APPLICATION

GOD'S DESIGN FOR MARRIAGE

The purpose for this handbook is to establish a firm foundation for marriage and provide the tools needed for a successful marital relationship, based on the principlesset out in the Word of God. It is our firm belief that couples should continue their marital education long after the wedding ceremony. This should include such things as reading books, attending seminars, couples' retreats.

> *"Except the LORD build the house, they labour in vain that build it: except the LORD keep the city, the watchman waketh but in vain."*[126]

I. GOD CREATED MARRIAGE TO BE BETWEEN ONE MAN AND ONE WOMAN - GENESIS 2:18-24

A. Marriage is a covenant - Genesis 17:2-11

Covenant - an agreement, usually formal, between two or more persons. The conditional promises made to humanity by God, as revealed in the scriptures.[127]

1. Do you understand the importance of covenant? (Explain in your own words.)

---

[125]Galatians 5:1 AMP
[126]Psalm 127:1 KJV
[127]Random House Dictionary, s.v. "covenant."

_____
_____
_____
_____

2. Are you ready to enter into covenant with your fiancé or potential mate? If so explain why? If not, why not?

_____
_____
_____
_____

B. God made woman from man for man. - Genesis 2:18; Proverbs 18:22

1. Do you believe that marriage was meant to be between a man and a woman? (Explain)

_____
_____
_____
_____

C. God designed marriage to be permanent. - Mark 10:9

1. Do you believe that marriage should be until death do you part? If so explain. If not, explain why not?

_____
_____
_____

_____

_____

II. ALL OTHER RELATIONSHIPS ARE TO BE SEVERED, ALTERED OR DROPPED. - MARK 10:7-9

Leave - to go away or depart. To stop, cease, abandon or exclude.'[128]

1. Do you have a close relationship with your parents? (If not, explain.)

_____
_____
_____
_____
_____

2. How do your parents feel about your potential mate? Did they give you their blessing? (If not, why not?)

_____
_____
_____
_____
_____

3. How do your potential mate's parents feel about you? Did they give you their blessing? (If not, why not?)

_____
_____

---

[128]Random House Dictionary Concise Edition April 1984

_____

_____

_____

4. Do you still live with your parents? (If so, why?)

_____

_____

_____

_____

_____

5. If you don't live at home, how long have you lived on your own? Do you live alone?

_____

_____

_____

_____

6. Do you pay your own bills? (List them.)

_____

_____

_____

_____

7. Do your friends like your mate? (If not, how close do you plan to be with these friends after the marriage?)

_____

_____

_____

_____

_____

8. After marriage, are you willing to leave home, family and friends to cleave to your mate? (If not, why not?)

_____

_____

_____

_____

_____

9. Are you willing to cut off all former relationships, including those with previous mates? (If not, why not?)

_____

_____

_____

_____

_____

III. CLEAVING IS A PROCESS OF TRANSFORMING YOUR THINKING TO CONSIDER YOUR MATE AND PUTTING THEIR NEEDS FIRST.

Cleave - to stick to, adhere to, catch by pursuit, to follow hard after, to hold close so that nothing can come in between [129]

1. Are you willing to make your mate your number one priority after God?

_____

[129]Definition for cleave is partially taken from The Amplified Bible and partially from Random House Dictionary, s.v. "cleave."

_____
_____
_____
_____
_____

2. Do you plan to have date nights and spend time doing things together as a couple regularly? How often?

_____
_____
_____
_____
_____

3. Are you willing to put the needs of your mate above your own needs?

_____
_____
_____

4. How often do you plan to spend time with family and friends? (holidays, birthdays, etc.?)

_____
_____
_____
_____
_____

5. Will you be living close to family? If so, why?

_____

_____

_____

_____

_____

IV. GOD'S WORD PROVIDES ALL THE TOOLS NEEDED TO BUILD A LOVING MARRIAGE .

"As His divine power has given to us all things that pertain to life and godliness, through the knowledge of Him who called us by glory and virtue,"[130]

A. Let God have control over who you are supposed to marry, and if you are supposed to marry prepare yourself.

1. Do you believe that you were led by the Spirit of God to your mate? (Explain how.)

_____

_____

_____

2. Do you believe that your mate has a strong relationship with God? (Explain.)

_____

_____

_____

_____

_____

[130]II Peter 1:3NKJV

V. A SUCCESSFUL MARRIAGE REQUIRES WISDOM - PROVERBS 24:3-4

"Through wisdom a house is built, and by understanding it is established; by knowledge the rooms are filled with all precious and pleasant riches." [131]

    A. Take offensive action to make your marriage strong.

        1. How often do you plan to attend marriage seminars, read books, go on retreats or participate in other activities to keep your marriage strong?

        _____

        _____

        _____

        _____

        _____

        2. Will you be accountable to another couple that can speak to you and your spouse regarding any marital problems you may have? (List their names.)

        If not, why not?

        _____

        _____

        _____

        _____

        _____

[131] Proverbs 24:3-4 NKJV

VI. A Successful Marriage Requires Work - Matthew 7:24-27

"Therefore whoever hears these sayings of Mine, and does them, I will liken him to a wise man who built his house on the rock: and the rain descended, the floods came, and the winds blew and beat on that house; and it did not fall, for it was founded on the rock. But everyone who hears these sayings of Mine, and does not do them, will be like a foolish man who built his house on the sand: and the rain descended, the floods came, and the winds blew and beat on that house; and it fell. And great was its fall."[132]

1. Are you willing to obey the Word of God and make it the final authority in your marriage—submitting to and adapting to one another out of reverence for God.[133]

2. Are you willing to die to selfishness and love your mate unconditionally?

CHAPTER 3 - PRACTICAL APPLICATION

BUILDING A STRONG FOUNDATION (LOVE)

I. BE IMITATORS OF THE LOVE OF GOD

A. Walk in unconditional love with your spouse - I Corinthians 13th Chapter

---

[132]Matthew 7:24-27 NKJV
[133]Ephesians 5:21-22 AMP

    1. Overcome the flesh by yielding to the Spirit. - Galatians 5:17-18; 2:20; 5:22-25

    2. Remember that love is an action word - I John 3:17-18

B. Put the five Greek ways to express love into practice:

    1. *Epithumia* - continue to express a strong desire for your mate.

    2. *Eros* - maintain the romance and emotional expression of the love you have for each other.

    3. *Storge* - the expression of your love for your family and friends changes.

    4. *Philae* - close friendships will change and new friendships with other couples should be developed.

    5. *Agape* - the God kind of love is required and this is the highest form of love. It is supernatural and unconditional. This love will keep you from sinning against each other. It will also cause you to love each other even when you don't feel like it.

C. Develop in the characteristics of God's love.

    1. God's love is immutable - Hebrews 6:18

    2. God's love is indestructible - I Corinthians 13:8

    3. God's love is inexhaustible - Matthew 18:22

II. Unconditional Love Survey

1. Love is patient - Reflect back on situations when you did not exhibit patience with your spouse and then list occasions when you can show love by walking in patience with him/her.

    _____

    _____

    _____

    _____

    _____

2. Love is kind - List ways you can show kindness on a continual basis (i.e. opening the car door, letting your spouse have the biggest donut, giving him/her flowers, picking up your dirty clothes, etc.).

    _____

    _____

    _____

    _____

    _____

3. Love is not jealous - Are you overly suspicious of your spouse? Do you always demand constant attention from him/her?

    _____

    _____

    _____

    _____

    _____

4. Love does not brag - Do you talk about yourself and what you do more than you show interest in what your spouse is doing?

What are ways you can lift up and encourage your spouse?

_____

_____

_____

_____

5. Love is not arrogant - Do you look down on your spouse's ideas, intellect, or decisions? Are your decisions always right, while your spouse's are always wrong? What practical ways can you value your spouse?

_____

_____

_____

_____

Love is not rude - How can you communicate your actions and words in a gentle way? The tongue of the wise brings healing.[134] Write out some phrases that would bring healing to your spouse.

_____

_____

_____

6. Love does not seek it's own - Are you primarily looking out for your needs, or are you seeking to discover your spouse's needs and attempting to fill them? Write down some of your spouse's needs.

_____

---

[134]Proverbs 12:18 AMP

_____
_____
_____

7. LOVE is not provoked - Do you experience angry outbursts? How should you respond when you attempt to put anger out in your spouse?

_____
_____
_____
_____
_____

8. Love doesn't take into account a suffered wrong - Do you recite a list of your spouse's past wrong doings that have already been dealt with when you have a disagreement with your spouse? We are to forgive in the same way that we have been forgiven by God. Write down four scriptures that deal with forgiveness, and pray them over your spouse.

_____
_____
_____
_____
_____

9. Walk in Agape Love - List ways you can improve in your walk of unconditional love with your spouse. (Romans 5:5; John 17:26; Galatians 5:22; II Corinthians 5:14; I John 4:16-17; John 1:12-13)

_____
_____

_____

_____

_____

CHAPTER 4 - PRACTICAL APPLICATION

COMPATIBILITY

"Do not be unequally yoked together with unbelievers. For what fellowship has righteousness with lawlessness? And what communion has light with darkness?"[135]

Compatible - capable of existing together in harmony.[136] -

I. THE SIGNS OF INCOMPATIBILITY

Examples of "red lights" or "major disagreements" that have not been resolved:

- Being unequally yoked with an unbeliever. - II Corinthians 6:14-15

- Not agreeing on what you believe salvation and being born again mean - John 3:16; Romans 5:8

- Not agreeing on whether you will have children - Genesis 9:1; Psalm 127:3-5

- Your ministry callings are very different; i.e. - you are called to overseas ministry and your potential spouse does not want to leave the United States.

---

[135]II Corinthians 6:14-15 - NKJV
[136]The Random House Dictionary Concise Edition 1989·

II. Personal Testimony & Spiritual Questionnaire

1. Are you born again, meaning you have received Jesus Christ as your personal Savior and Lord? - Romans 10:9-13

_____

_____

_____

_____

_____

2. What has your relationship with God been like? - St. John 12:26

_____

_____

_____

_____

_____

3. How did you come to the realization that you needed Jesus as your Savior? - John 14:6

_____

_____

_____

_____

_____

4. How often do you read the Bible and pray? - II Timothy 2:15; Luke 18:1

_____

_____

_____

_____

5. Do you attend church? If so, how often and where? - Hebrews 10:24-25; Matthew 12:9; Mark 12:21; Luke 4:16; Acts 13:14

_____

_____

_____

_____

6. Do you have a biblical approach to sexual purity before marriage? - Colossians 3:1-8

_____

_____

_____

_____

7. What are your beliefs about the Holy Spirit? - Romans 14:16-26 & Acts 1:8

_____

_____

_____

8. Do you speak in other tongues? If so, why? If not, why not? - Acts Chapter 2

_____

_____

_____

---

9. Do you tithe and give offerings? If so, why? If not, why not? - Malachi 3:8-12; Genesis 14:18-20; Hebrews 7:4-8; Luke 6:38; II Corinthians 9:6-10

_____

_____

_____

_____

10. Do you believe in the gifts of the Spirit? - Ephesians 4:11-13; Romans 12:1-12; I Corinthians 12:1-14; Mark 16:15-18

_____

_____

_____

11. What are your natural gifts and talents?

_____

_____

_____

_____

12. Do you believe in praying for guidance when it comes to choosing a mate?

_____

_____

_____

_____

13. Do you believe in fasting?

_____

_____

_____

_____

_____

_____

14. Have you fasted about your relationship with the person to whom you are engaged to?

_____

_____

_____

_____

15. Do you believe the following are acceptable for a Christian to participate in? (Check √ for "yes")

__ social drinking   __ drinking at home   __ drinking only away from home   __ **R**-rated movies   __ pornography   __ smoking __ watching TV   __ going to clubs   __ having an affair while married __marrying more than one wife   __ living together before marriage

16. Were you raised in church? If so, what denomination?

_____

_____

_____

_____

17. How do you feel about birth control?   Abortion?

_____

_____

_____

_____

_____

18. Do you enjoy fellowshipping with other Christians? How Often?

_____

_____

_____

_____

_____

19. Are you involved in ministry at your church? In what area and for how long? Ephesians 4:11-12

_____

_____

_____

_____

_____

20. After you are married, do you plan to continue to be involved in this area of ministry or some other area?

_____

_____

_____

_____

_____

21. Have you totally agreed on what church you will attend after you are married?   If not, how will you go about deciding this after you are married?

_____

_____

_____

_____

_____

22. Do you feel like you are called to full-time ministry? If so, what area of ministry?

_____

_____

_____

_____

_____

23. Do you know what your fiancé's ministry calling is?

_____

_____

_____

_____

_____

24. What do you plan to do to help him/her reach their goals?

_____

_____

_____

_____

25. Will you have weekly family devotions? If so, who will lead them?

_____

_____

_____

_____

26. What role do you believe your pastor plays in your life?

_____

_____

_____

_____

27. Do you believe God speaks to you through your pastor?

_____

_____

_____

_____

28. Do you believe God has placed leadership in the church to help you?

_____

_____

_____

_____

29. Do you believe you are spiritually accountable to the leadership in your church?

_____

_____

_____

_____

30. Do you plan to have a ministry with your spouse after you are married, or do you plan to work in separate areas of the church?

_____

_____

_____

_____

31. Do you feel the church takes away your time, or do you believe the church offers you an opportunity to serve God?

_____

_____

_____

_____

32. Do you plan to change any of your spiritual habits after marriage? List what you specifically do not want to change, i.e. prayer times, etc.:

_____

_____

_____

_____

33. Do you and your future mate have prayer time together now? How often?

_____

_____

_____

_____

_____

34. Do you feel uncomfortable praying with your future mate? If so why?

_____

_____

_____

35. How do you know that your future plans are God's will for your life?

_____

_____

_____

_____

III. BIBLE DOCTRINE (CORE BELIEFS)

1. Do you believe that Jesus Christ is the only way to salvation?

2. Do you believe in divine healing?

3. If, after marriage, you, your spouse or your child become ill, what is the first thing you would do?

4. Would you take your sick child to the doctor if necessary?

5. Would you allow your spouse to see a doctor if he or she is ill?

6. Do you believe the Bible is the inspired Word of God?

7. Do you accept the Bible as the final authority in your life?

8. Would you be willing to obey the Bible, even though it might require you to do something you did not want to do?

9. Do you discuss the Bible with your future mate?

10. How do you handle differences of opinion about Bible doctrines?

11. Are you familiar with the Statement of Faith of the church you now attend?

12. Have you discussed the Statement of Faith of your church with your future mate?

13. Do you pay tithes now? Do you plan to continue to pay tithes after you get married?

14. Do you believe hospitality and fellowship is a part of Christianity?

15. What would you do (after marriage) if the pastor where you attend church began to teach doctrines you did not believe were in line with the Bible?

IV. LEARNING TO HANDLE DIFFERENCES

1. How would you resolve differences of spiritual beliefs between you and your mate after?

_____

_____

_____

_____

2. Would you initiate and/or be willing to go to a Christian counselor if you were having marital disagreements?

_____

_____

_____

_____

3. Where would you seek counseling? (Church, private psychologist, therapist, friend, etc.)

_____

_____

_____

_____

4. Do you know what the Bible says about marriage and divorce?

_____

_____

_____

5. Are you willing to abide by what the Bible says about marriage and divorce?

_____

_____

_____

6. How would you handle it if you felt your spouse was spending too much time in spiritual matters (prayer, church attendance, church related activities, etc.)?

_____

_____

_____

_____

7. How would you handle it if your spouse slowly quit going to church with you, and began showing a lack of interest in spiritual matters?

_____

_____

_____

_____

8. What would you do if your spouse was trying to coerce (force) you into doing something you felt you absolutely could not do?

_____

_____

_____

_____

9. Do you believe one spouse should coerce (force) the other one to do anything, either openly or subtly?

_____

_____

_____

_____

10.Describe what you believe "submission" means.

_____

_____

_____

_____

V. Know No Man or Woman After the Flesh - II Corinthians 5:16

1. Do you believe you can judge a person by what they look like?

2. How much time do you believe it takes to get to know someone?

3. Do you believe it is important to become friends first, before considering someone as a potential mate?

4. Do you believe that God will lead you to the right person and/or bring that person to you?

5. Do you realize the importance of not looking for the right person but being the right person?

6. How do you know someone by the spirit? (i.e. praying together, talking about the word of God, seeing what fruits of the spirit and gifts of the spirit operate in their life?)

VI. Find Your Personality Type

A. Take a personality test to determinewhat you and your potential mates personality types are.

B. Your personality type is not an excuse to disobey the Word of God.

C. Learn to balance the hard and soft side of love.

D. Jesus was a perfect balance of every personality type.

   1. He was decisive and took charge. - Matthew 21:10-13

   2. He was sociable and popular - John 2:1-9; Matthew 11:19

   3. He was disciplined and detailed - Matthew 5:17; John 8:28-29

   4. He was nurturing and compassionate - Matthew 9:36; Matt. 14:14

E. Make yourselves accountable to your parents prior to marriage andafter marriage, have accountability partners in your life who can help you work on personality problems.

STATEMENT OF FAITH

1. ONE TRUE GOD: God has revealed Himself as the eternally self-existent I AM, the Creator of all things and redeemer of mankind who is infinitely perfect and manifests as Father, Son and Holy Spirit (Isaiah 43:11, Luke 3:33).

2. THE INSPIRED SCRIPTURES: The scriptures, Old and New Testaments, are the inspired Word of God, the revelation of God to man, and the infallible, final authority for all Christian faith and practice (II Timothy 3:15-17).

3. THE DEITY OF JESUS CHRIST: The Lord Jesus Christ is the eternal Son of God and shares the Deity of God. He is also truly man, conceived of the Holy Spirit, born of a virgin Mary, died on the cross as the sacrifice for sin, arose from the dead, ascended into Heaven, and is now at the right hand of the Father as our High Priest and Advocate (Matthew 1:23).

4. ORIGINAL SIN AND THE FALL OF MAN: Man was created in the image of God but disobeyed and fell from the grace of God. From this fall, sin entered the world and brought death by sin, causing not only physical death but spiritual death (Genesis 1-3).

5. SALVATION BY FAITH: Man sins because he has a sinful nature. Only through the shed blood of Jesus Christ and His resurrection can man find salvation from the power of sin. This salvation and spiritual life, a free gift of grace from God, can only be obtained by exercising faith in the person and finished work of the Lord Jesus Christ (Ephesians 2:8-9).

6. THE NEW MAN IN CHRIST: If any man be in Christ, he is a new creature (creation) in the inward man. We are His workmanship created in Christ Jesus. We are partakers of His divine nature (II Corinthians 5:17; Ephesians 2:10; II Peter 1:4).

7. BAPTISM IN THE HOLY SPIRIT: The baptism in the Holy Spirit is to glorify Jesus Christ and to indwell, guide and empower believers for life and service. This baptism brings the gifts or enablements of the Holy Spirit and their uses to the forefront of the ministry of the Body of Christ. This experience is distinct from and subsequent to the experience of the new birth and is evidence by the initial physical sign of speaking with other tongues as the Spirit of God gives utterance (Acts 1-4).

8. DIVINE HEALING: The redemption provided by Jesus Christ includes more than just forgiveness of sins. Healing is also an integral part of the Gospel (Matthew 8:16-17; James 5:14-16).

9. THE CHURCH - THE BODY OF CHRIST: Christ's Church, made up of born-again believers, is God's habitation through the Holy Spirit. When believers are born of the Spirit, they are united together as the Body of Christ and appointed to fulfill the great commission. Jesus Christ is both Lord and head of His Church (Ephesians 1:22-23).

10. THE SACRAMENTS OF THE CHURCH:

    A. **Baptism in water:** All who believe in Christ Jesus as their Lord and Savior are commanded to be immersed in water, as a declaration that they have identified with the death of Christ and have been raised with Him in newness of life (Mark 16:16; Acts 10:47-48).

B. **The Lord's Supper:** Communion is a symbolic expression of our sharing the divine nature of the Lord Jesus Christ (2 Peter 1:4), as well as a memorial of His suffering and death. It is also a prophecy of His second coming (I Corinthians 11:23-31).

11. RESURRECTION OF THE SAINTS: One day coming, the entire Body of Christ will be caught up together to meet the Lord in the air; and so shall we ever be with the Lord (I Thessalonians 4:13-18).

12. THE SECOND COMING OF CHRIST: The Second Coming of Christ is the actual, visible return of Christ to establish His Kingdom (Matthew 24:27-30). It will include the catching away of the Church (I Thessalonians 4:16-17), followed by the visible return of Christ with His saints (the Church) to reign with Him on earth for one thousand years (Zechariah 14:5; Revelation 1:7; 19:11-15; 20:1-6). The millennial reign will bring the salvation of national Israel and the establishment of universal peace.

13. THE FINAL JUDGEMENT: There will be a day when the wicked dead will be   raised and judged according to their works. Whosoever is not found written in the Lamb's Book of Life will be sentenced to everlasting punishment in the Lake of Fire (Revelation 20:11-15).

Chapter 5 - PRACTICAL APPLICATION

ROLES IN MARRIAGE

I. The Relationship Between Husband and Wife = Christ & The Church

A. The husband is to be like Christ - *Giving*

B. The wife is to be like the church - *Reflecting*

II. The Husband's Role: Man Was Created to be a Leader - Ephesians 5:23-26

> *"And the LORD God caused a deep sleep to fall on Adam, and he slept; and He took one of his ribs, and closed up the flesh in its place. Then the rib which the LORD God had taken from man He made into a woman, and He brought her to the man. And Adam said, 'This is now bone of my bones and flesh of my flesh; she shall be called Woman, because she was taken out of Man.' Therefore a man shall leave his father and mother and be joined to his wife, and they shall become one flesh."[137]*

A. The husband is called to serve.

1. The husband is to demonstrate God's love toward his wife.

2. The husband is to be his wife's protector.

3. He is to keep God first in his life.

4. He is to speak God's Word over his wife.

[137] *Genesis 2:21-24 - NKJV*

5. The husband should be the first to leave his father and mother's home to prepare for marriage.

6. The husband should be the leader in hearing God's direction for his household.

B. The husband must learn how to meet the needs of his wife.

1. Knowing when your wife needs your shoulder, not your mouth.

2. A man must know how to give his wife attention and affection.

3. Men must know how to make a thoughtful request, instead of a selfish demand.

III. THE WIFE'S ROLE: WOMAN WAS MADE FROM MAN FOR MAN - GENESIS 2:18

"And the LORD God said, 'It is not good that man should be alone; I will make him a helper comparable to him'.[138]

A. Woman was created to be man's helper - Genesis 2:18; Esther 4:1517; 5:1-8; 7:1-8; Proverbs 31:10-29God has gifted the woman with insight; the ability to help man accomplish the vision God has placed in him.

1. She is a helper spiritually

2. She is a helper emotionally

3. She is a helper financially

B. God gave the wife a position of submission - Ephesians 5:21-22

<u>Submit</u> - to yield (oneself) to the power of another. To present for consideration. To present as an opinion. To comply, obey, surrender.[139]

---

[138]Genesis 2:18
[139]Random House Dictionary, s.v. "submit".

C. Submission also means adapting to, respecting and honoring your husband - Ephesians 5:33; I Peter 3:1.

<u>Respect</u> - High admiration or esteem for a person or quality. To show regard or consideration. Notices, honors, regards, venerates, esteems, prefers, defers to, praises, loves and admires.[140]

1. Be your husband's #1 cheerleader!

2. Get behind his dreams.

3. Verbalize appreciation for who he is and all he does.

4. Keep your husband covered with prayer.

D. The wife is to be a woman of virtue - Titus 2:4-5; Proverbs 12:4; 18:22: 19:14; I Timothy 3:11.

"...the older women likewise, that they be reverent in behavior, not slanderers, not given to much wine, teachers of good things— that they admonish the young women to love their husbands, to love their children, to be discreet, chaste, homemakers, good, obedient to their own husbands, that the word of God may not be blasphemed." [141]

---

[140]Ibid, s.v. "respect".
[141]Titus 2:4-5 - NKJV

Chapter 6 - Practical Application

MEETING EACH OTHERS NEEDS

"For you, brethren, have been called to liberty; only do not use liberty as an opportunity for the flesh, but through love serve one another."[142]

I. Dwell with One Another with Knowledge - I Peter 3:7

"Likewise, ye husbands, dwell with them according to knowledge, giving honour unto the wife, as unto the weaker vessel, and as being heirs together of the grace of life; that your prayers be not hindered."[143] -

A. We must take the time to find out what our spouses needs are.

B. Recognize the difference between a spiritual need and a natural need.

C. Don't try to make your spouse meet your needs, but look to the Lord to meet your own needs. - Phillipians 4:19.

D. Husbands and wives must have a servant attitude toward each other.

II. Meeting the Needs of Your Wife

A. The physical makeup of a woman is different than the physical make-up of a man.

---

[142]Galatians 5:13 NKJV
[143]KJV

134

1. She needs time for rest and relaxation: Understand that she enjoys taking time to renew her emotional and physical well-being. Take time to go on walks with her, give her time alone to read books, take long baths, pamper her with massages and foot rubs, take time for cuddling with her, and spend at least one relaxing evening at home with her each week.

2. She needs you to be open and honest: Tell her everything about yourself, leaving nothing out that might later surprise her. Describe your positive and negative feelings, events of your past, daily schedule, and plans for the future. Do not confuse demands, disrespect, or anger with honesty. Be respectful whenever your opinions differ. Take interest in knowing about her feelings, events of her past, her daily schedule, and her plans for the future.

3. She needs affection: Tell her you love her and care for her with words, cards, flowers, gifts and common courtesies. Give her hugs and kisses several times a day, creating an environment of affection that clearly and repeatedly expresses your love and care for her.

4. She needs conversation: Set aside time each day just to talk to her. Talk with her about events in your lives, your children, your feelings, and your plans. Whatever the topic, avoid demands, disrespect, or anger, and don't dwell on her mistakes. When you talk to her, give her your undivided attention and make sure you both contribute equally to the conversation.

5. She needs financial security: Assume responsibility to house, feed, and clothe your family. If your income is in-

sufficient to provide essential support, be willing to up-grade your skills to provide that support without having to work long hours that would keep you from her and your children. Encourage her to pursue a career, but do not depend on her salary for basic family expenses.

6. She needs commitment to the family and a dedicated fa-ther to her children: Commit sufficient time and energy to the moral and educational development of your chil-dren. Read to them, engage in sports with them, and take them on frequent outings. Also, read books and attend lectures with her on the subject of child development so you will both do a good job training your children. Dis-cuss training methods and objectives with her until you both agree, and you do not proceed with any plan of dis-cipline without her approval. Recognize that the happi-ness and success of your children is critically important to her.

III. MEETING THE NEEDS OF YOUR HUSBAND

The care and emotional needs of a man are different than those of a woman.

1. A wife needs to understand her husband's need for sex-ual fulfillment: Meet this need by being a terrific sexual partner for him. Study your own response to recognize and understand what brings the best out in you sexually. Share this information with your husband, so together you can learn to have a sexual relationship that is as fre-quent as he wants, yet enjoyable for both of you.

2. He needs an attractive and healthy wife: Keep yourself

physically fit with diet and exercise and wear your hair, makeup, and clothes in a way that he finds attractive and tasteful. He will be attracted to you in private and proud of you in public.

3. He needs domestic tranquility: Create a home environment that offers him a refuge from the stresses of life. Manage the household responsibilities in a way that encourages him to spend time at home, enjoying his family.

4. She needs to understand his need for respect: Be proud of him, not out of duty, but from a profound respect for the man you chose to marry. Remind him of his value and achievements and help him maintain self-confidence. Avoid criticizing him.

5. She needs to be the one who meets his need for admiration: Understand and appreciate him more than anyone else does. Constantly tell him that you believe in him. Help him achieve his dreams and goals. Remember, you are his number one cheerleader.

6. He needs recreational companionship: Develop an interest in the recreational activities that he enjoys the most and try to become proficient at them. If you find that you cannot enjoy these activities, encourage him to consider other activities that you both can enjoy together. You are his favorite recreational companion, and he associates you with his most enjoyable moments of relaxation.

IV. HUSBAND'S & WIFE'S EMOTIONAL NEEDS

From the list below, choose your top five most important emotional needs and list them in the order of priority; sign and date. Exchange this list with your spouse or potential mate.

1. Admiration

2. Affection

3. Respect

4. Conversation

5. Financial Security

6. Domestic Tranquility

7. Commitment to Family

8. Openness & Honesty

9. Physical Attractiveness

10. Sexual Fulfillment

11. Recreational Companionship

12. Time for Rest & Relaxation

1. _____

2. _____

3. _____

4. _____

5. _____

Name_____

Date_____

CHAPTER 7 - PRACTICAL APPLICATION

THE BASICS ON FINANCES

"And if you are untrustworthy about worldly wealth, who will trust you with the true riches of heaven? And if you are not faithful with other people's things, why should you be trusted with things of your own?"[144]

I. CREATE A SPENDING PLAN: Basic Sample:

Income	$
Tithes	$
Offerings	$
Bills	$
Savings/Investment	$
Food	$
Clothing	$
Medical Expenses	$
Insurance: Health, Life, Home, Car, Boat, etc.	$
Entertainment/ Recreation	$
Discretionary Funds	$
Miscellaneous Funds	$

---

[144]Luke 16:11-12 NLT

1. Income: Your total earnings after taxes.[145]

2. Tithes: 10% of your gross income.[146]

3. Offerings: Money given over and above the tithe as you purpose in your heart to give.[147]

4. Bills: Mortgage, rent, utilities, car payments, etc.

5. Savings/Investment: A percentage of your income put away each pay or monthly in a savings account and/or money invested in stocks, bonds, mutual funds, 401k, etc.

6. Food: Weekly or monthly food expenses; including restaurants.

7. Clothing: Monthly clothing expenses, purchased as needed.

8. Medical Expenses: Money put away monthly to cover annual or unexpected doctor visits, dental, vision, etc.

9. Insurance; Health & Life: Money if not taken out by employer, that is paid to cover a Health & Life insurance policy.

10. Insurance; Home, Car, Boat, etc: Money paid to cover your home, car, boat, etc., against damages.

11. Entertainment/Recreation: Movies, games, internet, cable, date night and any other recreational activities.

12. Discretionary Funds: An allowance or money for each of you to use at your discretion. (i.e. surprise gifts, lunches, etc.)

13. Miscellaneous Funds: haircuts, gym fees, manicures, makeup, etc.

---

[145]Matthew 17:27 KJV; Matthew 22:21 KJV
[146]Malachi 3:10 KJV; Genesis 28:22 KJV; Proverbs 3:9 KJV, Hebrews 7:8 KJV
[147]II Corinthians 9:6-7 KJV; Luke 6:38 KJV

II. HUSBANDS AND WIVES MUST BE IN UNITY CONCERNING THEIR FINANCES

"Make every effort to keep the unity of the Spirit through the bond of peace."[148]

1. What is your personal background and beliefs about money? (i.e. How your parents spent money)

_____
_____
_____
_____
_____

2. What are your spending habits like? (i.e. Are you a bargain hunter? Do you look at the price of what you buy or do you just buy what you want?)

_____
_____
_____
_____
_____

3. Do you have debts and have you created a plan to pay them off? (List and explain.)

_____
_____
_____
_____
_____

[148]Ephesians 4:3 AMP

4. Will you strive to maintain unity between you and your mate when it comes to finances? How will you achieve this unity?

_____

_____

_____

_____

_____

5. Will you keep a separate bank account? If so, why?

_____

_____

_____

_____

_____

6. After you are married, will it be: (choose one)

   a) my money

   b) your money

   c) our money

7. Who will keep the checkbook and/or pay the bills? (Remember, both of you should have access to this information.)

_____

_____

_____

_____

_____

III. FINANCIAL AGREEMENT

I hereby agree to allow God to be the head of our finances and I will be a faithful steward of the blessings that the Lord has bestowed on us. I will walk in unity and financial integrity with God, my spouse and others. We will owe no man anything but love. *"Keep out of debt and owe no man anything, except to love one another; for he who loves his neighbor [who practices loving others] has fulfilled the Law [relating to one's fellowmen, meeting all its requirements]."*[149]

_____

Husband's Signature

_____

Wife's Signature

---

[149]Romans 13:8 AMP

CHAPTER 8 - PRACTICAL APPLICATION

COMMUNICATION GUIDELINES

"Understand [this], my beloved brethren. Let every man be quick to hear [a ready listener], slow to speak, slow to take offense and to get angry. For man's anger does not promote the righteousness God [wishes and requires]. So get rid of all uncleanness and the rampant outgrowth of wickedness, and in a humble (gentle, modest) spirit receive and welcome the Word which implanted and rooted [in your hearts] contains the power to save your souls."[150]

In humility, receive the Word implanted, which is able to save your marriage. Humility gives up the right to be right (Charity). Take the time it requires to build a strong relationship with good communication and mix it with the fruit of the Spirit (Carl).

COMMUNICATION QUESTIONNAIRE:

1. A good listener will not be _____ while their spouse is still talking.[151]

    a. sleeping

    b. thinking of a response

    c. watching football

    d. all of the above

---

[150]James 1:19-21 AMP
[151]Proverbs 18:13 KJV

2. Listening involves _____.

    a. hearing

    b. good posture

    c. good eye contact

3. Look below the _____ of what is being said.

    a. surface

    b. matter at hand

    c. feelings

4. Create an atmosphere of _____.

    a. acceptance

    b. freedom to communicate

    c. good will

    d. all of the above

5. Give your _____ and repeat what is being said. You are telling your spouse that they are valuable.

    a. best effort

    b. honest opinion

    c. full attention

6. Include_____ listening in your communication. Make sure the message being communicated is the message received.

    a. good

    b. reflective

    c. total

7. A proper listener will not _____ but will _____. Don't be led by your emotions.

    a. think/talk

    b. judge/listen

    c. react/respond

8. List the five levels of communication:

    1) _____

    2) _____

    3) _____

    4) _____

    5) _____

9. What level of communication are you on with your spouse or potential mate? _____

10. Be a _____ and do not answer until the other person has finished.[152]

    a. ready listener

---

[152]James 1:19; Proverbs 18:13 KJV

b. humble person

c. smart person

d. all of the above

11. Be slow _____. Do not be hasty in your word choices. Don't blurt out every thought that comes to your mind. Words cannot be taken back once they are spoken.[153]

a. to get angry

b. to speak

c. to react

12. Speak the truth in _____, even when expressing an irritation or annoyance. Wait until you can speak in the right spirit.[154]

a. love

b. all honesty

c. humility

13. Get the _____ out of your own eye before getting the _____ out of the eye of your spouse.[155]

a. lint/dust

b. log/splinter

c. beam/mote

[153]Proverbs 15:28; 21:23; 29:20 AMP
[154]Ephesians 4:15 AMP
[155]Matthew 7:5 KJV

14. Do not give the _____ treatment or the cold shoulder.[156] This is a form of punishment. We must choose to put an end to strife.

    a. silent

    b. wrong

    c. cold

15. Do not _____ or argue. It takes two to argue but only one to put it out.[157] Don't give in to the works of the flesh. This destroys romantic love, self esteem and the security in our relationships.

    a. shout

    b. quarrel

    c. fight

    d. all of the above

16. A _____ will turn away anger. Do not react in anger but be controlled by the Holy Spirit.[158] Do not grieve the Holy Spirit. Pray and then respond with the wisdom of the Holy Spirit.

    a. smart answer

    b. soft answer

    c. right answer

[156]Ephesians 4:26 NLT
[157]James 4:1; Ephesians 4:31 KJV
[158]Proverbs 15:1; Ephesians 4:29-32 KJV

17. _____ and admit when you have been wrong our hurtful.[159]

    a. Humble yourself

    b. Make excuses

    c. Be careful

18. Avoid _____.[160]

    a. arguing

    b. yelling

    c. nagging

    d. all of the above

19. Don't _____ or _____ the other person. If you are verbally attacked or criticized, don't respond in like manner.[161]

    a. blame/criticize

    b. attack/ridicule

    c. ignore/belittle

    d. all of the above

20. Try to understand the other's _____ and make allowance for differences.[162]

    a. feelings

    b. point of view

---

[159]Ephesians 4:32; James 4:10: Proverbs 26:3-12 AMP
[160]Proverbs 10:19; 17:9; 20:5 KJV
[161]I Peter 3:8-9; Romans 12:17 AMP
[162]Philippians 2:1-4; Ephesians 4:2 AMP

    c. opinion

    d. all of the above

21. Adopt a _____ _____ strategy.

    a. two winner

    b. one topic

    c. sure fire

22. Stay on one _____ at a time and resolve it.

    a. subject

    b. topic

    c. problem

    d. all of the above

23. Own your own _____. Use "I" messages instead of "You" messages.

    a. feelings

    b. habits

    c. ideas

24. Do not bring up an issue of _____ or a list, when it has already been dealt with.[163]

    a. hurt feelings

    b. the past

    c. unresolved problems

---

[163]I Corinthians 13:5; I Peter 4:8 AMP

25. Do not _____ your spouse's actions (i.e. "You always" or "You never." This builds defensiveness.)

    a. exaggerate

    b. imitate

    c. generalize

26. Always give _____ before displeasure.

    a. respect

    b. a reason

    c. acceptance

27. Define what is _____ _____ and what is hitting below the belt. Things that cannot be brought up.

    a. too harsh

    b. off limits

    c. not allowed

    d. all of the above

28. Commit to _____ without _____. Acknowledge what was said and ask questions.

    a. hearing/speaking

    b. listening/interrupting

    c. speaking/thinking

    d. both a and b.

29. Ask what _____ your spouse would like to see. (Don't do this in the midst of a disagreement.)

    a. improvements

    b. changes

    c. progress

    d. all of the above

30. Allow the _____ of the Spirit to flow when a disagreement arises. No yelling or uncontrolled anger (use self-control).[164]

    a. peace

    b. fruit

    c. kindness

    d. all of the above

31. If _____ person wants to discuss an issue, then it is important enough to be discussed. Don't belittle your mate's feelings.

    a. one

    b. either

    c. any

    d. all of the above

32. _____ is inappropriate. Don't make jokes about your spouse, especially in public.

    a. Criticism

    b. Sarcasm

[164] Galatians 5:18,25, NLT

    c. Lying

33. _____ for your spouse and ask the Holy Spirit to change you as well as your spouse.

    a. Live

    b. Pray

    c. Speak

34. Don't wait for your spouse to respond in love _____. Walk in unconditional love and be the initiator of peace.[165]

    a. first

    b. second

    c. last

    d. all of the above

I choose to honor my spouse by following these guidelines.

Name_____ Date_____

Name_____ Date_____

---

[165] I Corinthians 14:1 KJV

COMMUNICATION TESTIMONIAL:

We want to share the following testimonies as a living example of putting the correct communication into action in your marital relationship. This beautiful couple is from Kenya and has been married for about four years.

ESTER'S TESTIMONY:

It was on a Friday when my husband and I decided to go for an all night prayer at Victory Christian Center church. The prayers normally start from 10pm to 6am. During prayers at about 3 am in the morning, my husband was getting sleepy and he wanted to go home but I wanted to stay because I felt I had more energy to pray and the meeting was very anointed. My husband actually told me we could go home and I could continue to pray from the house but I declined. So we agreed that I should give him the house keys since we had only carried one pair and that he would not lock the house so I would not have to wake him up when I got to the house.

This was during winter because when I left at 6 am it was still dark. To my surprise when I got to the house, I found the door locked!! I knocked several times, tried calling him, screamed out his name, banged the window, with no response. By this time, I was getting so upset with him because I did not understand how he could lock me out. For me this was unacceptable. I tried to imagine if we had children would he have locked them out. At the time, what came to me was that he does not care about me that much and all he thinks of is himself. I felt so insecure, rejected and betrayed. I had no choice but to go back into the car and drive to church and wait until probably later when I would have to try again.

When I got into the car I wanted to make one more call again and I realized my battery for the phone was dead. I sat there feeling so frustrated then I saw a neighbor of mine who had just finished talking on the phone so I decided to ask him for his phone so I could try and call my husband again. Fortunately my husband picked up the phone and the first thing I did was to yell at him how could he dare lock me out!! I could not reason with him because I was so mad. As I was getting ready to get to the house I gave that man his phone and told him Jesus loves him and he turned against me trying to make passes at me which was unbelievable! And I realized how the enemy waits when you are at the lowest point and attacks you!

Later when I spoke to my husband and listened to his side of the story and with the help of our accountability partners (Pastors Charity and Carl) I realized that my husband did not do this intentionally, he was sincere and that he actually just forgot. He was so tired and went to bed thinking that he did not lock the door. This experience made me realize I really didn't know my husband and that I was not secure in his love and didn't trust that he loved me. If I was secure that he loved me then I would not have reacted the way I did. I would have known that he would never do that and I would have instead responded that he just forgot and it's not a big deal. I then began working on how to trust him and know that he is there for me and not against me. This also revealed to me that there are things from my past relationships that I had to deal with and heal from.

Ester Lilian Matu

JOEL'S TESTIMONY:

It was on a Friday night, my wife and I had gone for an all night prayer at our local church that started at 10 pm and ended at 6 am. At around 3 am I found myself getting sleepy; I was tired and wanted to go home. I told my wife that we should leave and she could continue the prayer at home, she replied to me that she was feeling the presence of the Lord in the church and wanted to stay longer until the prayer ended.

We then agreed that I should leave her with the car, and get a ride home from a friend of mine who was at the prayer, and was also leaving at the same time. I took the house keys, and promised my wife that I would make sure that I left the front door open; so that when she comes in she will not have to wake me up (this was because, I knew that I would probably be in deep sleep). My friend dropped me at home, but I was so tired that for some reason I forgot to leave the front door open. I went to sleep and at around 7am I woke to the sound of my phone ringing, it was my wife on the other end of the line and she sounded very upset.

At this point she was shouting at me "How could you leave the door closed, I've been trying to call you, I am scared, there is a man outside who has been approaching me" my wife was upset and frantic. I told her that "I didn't lock the door" (cause I thought that I had left the door open). I checked the door and it was locked and I was so shocked, I must have locked it as a reflex action. There were also a number of missed calls from my wife's phone, I knew I was in trouble.

I opened the door and she was very upset, she continuously told me that" I need to be more responsible". This was a "bad mistake" and it took a while for my wife to let go of this one. Later on we spoke to our accountability marriage couple the Taylor's, and we explained to them the story. The first thing that they told me was I should have never left my wife alone at the prayer, couples are supposed to be together, and men are supposed to protect their wives. Carl Taylor's words were "Men are supposed to protect their wives, how are you going to protect your spouse when you are at home, and she is outside". I received that rebuke, they also told us that my wife should have agreed to come home with me, because God would have honored her submission, and the presence of the Lord can be very much at your home as it is at the church. I learnt a big lesson through this mistake, first men are supposed to protect their wives, and we should never leave our wives alone especially at night. I also learned that I should have sacrificed my sleep to be with my wife that night, and that is the love of Christ.

Joel Matu

CHAPTER 9 - PRACTICAL APPLICATION

GOD'S PLAN FOR THE MARRIAGE BED

"And the rib or part of his side which the Lord God had taken from the man He built up and made into a woman, and He brought her to the man. Then Adam said, This [creature] is now bone of my bones and flesh of my flesh; she shall be called Woman, because she was taken out of a man. Therefore a man shall leave his father and his mother and shall become united and cleave to his wife, and they shall become one flesh. And the man and his wife were both naked and were not embarrassed or ashamed in each other's presence."[166]

---

[166]Genesis 2:22-25 AMP

1. What is your attitude toward sex?

    a. List the negatives - (i.e. wrong teaching, sexual abuse, premarital sex, shame or guilt). -

    _____

    _____

    _____

    _____

    _____

    _____

    _____

    b. List the positives - (i.e. No shame, cleaving, sexual unity).

    _____

    _____

    _____

    _____

    _____

    _____

    _____

2. God is the _____ of the marriage union.

    a. author

    b. creator

    c. designer

    d. all of the above

3. Sex is not just physical, it is _____.

    a. emotional

b. intellectual

c. an expression of affection

d. intimacy

e. all of the above

4. Sexual unity fulfills several purposes: _____.

   a. Procreation

   b. Unity

   c. Mutual Pleasure

   d. all of the above

5. Sexual unity is an _____.

   a. outward sign of an inward bond

   b. a time of concentrating on each other

   c. part of cleaving

   d. all of the above

6. Your bodies _____.

   a. are not your own

   b. belong to each other

   c. belong to God

   d. all of the above

7. Don't _____ each other of habitual lovemaking.

   a. deprive

b. defraud

c. neglect

d. all of the above

8. Explain how each of these barriers effect your ability to experience blessed marriage bed.

a. The past -

_____

_____

_____

_____

_____

b. Vain imaginations -

_____

_____

_____

_____

_____

c. Lack of desire -

_____

_____

_____

_____

_____

d. Anger/Disagreements -

_____

PRACTICAL APPLICATION MANUAL

_____

_____

_____

_____

e. Selfishness -

_____

_____

_____

_____

f. Not understanding the difference between men and women and their arousals -

_____

_____

_____

_____

g. Time -

_____

_____

_____

_____

h. Birth Control -

_____

_____

_____

_____

_____

i. Distractions -

_____

_____

_____

_____

_____

j. The Privacy factor -

_____

_____

_____

_____

_____

k. Lack of Variety -

_____

_____

_____

_____

_____

CHAPTER 10 - PRACTICAL APPLICATION

BUILDING HEDGES AROUND YOUR MARRIAGE

"Have You not put a hedge about him and his house and all that he has, on every side? You have conferred prosperity and happiness upon him in the work of his hands, and his possessions have increased in the land."[167]

HEDGE# 1: UNCONDITIONAL LOVE

"Watch over your heart with all diligence, for from it flow the springs of life."[168]

Diligence - constant in effort to accomplish something.[169]

It is going to take a constant effort to not allow your emotions to control you, but to allow the love of God to guard over and protect your heart.

1. _____ chapter is the pattern for walking in unconditional love.

2. _____ gives of itself without expecting anything in return.

3. Unless you walk in _____, your love will never grow or develop the way God intended it to.

4. Love grows in times of _____.

5. When love is tested it manifests the _____.

6. When selfishness is tested it manifests the _____.

[167]Job 1:10 AMP
[168]Proverbs 4:23 NASB
The Random House Dictionary Concise Edition, s.v. "diligence".

7. If you are led by your emotions, you will always be _____.

8. Love is not based on emotions, it is a _____.

9. God wants us to follow His _____.

10. It takes _____ to adapt to the differences in each other's personalities.

11. Unconditional love gives you the _____ and _____ to make the necessary adjustments to accommodate these differences.

12. Remember that you are not just _____ in to your spouse, but you are _____ to God.

HEDGE# 2: PRAYER & CONFESSING GOD'S WORD OVER YOUR SPOUSE

> *"Husbands, love your wives, just as Christ also loved the church and gave Himself for her, that He might sanctify and cleanse her with the washing of water by the word, that He might present her to Himself a glorious church, not having spot or wrinkle or any such thing, but that she should be holy and without blemish."*[170]

Remember that you will have what you say, and that is why it is so important to speak what God's Word says, over your spouse *(Mark 11:23-25)*.

1. Don't allow your _____ to control what you say about your spouse.

2. Be willing to walk in _____, even if your spouse doesn't

---

[170]Ephesians 5:25-27 NKJV

ask to be _____.

3. It is so important not to be quick to get _____ or _____.

4. It is so important to get to know each other by the _____ first.

5. In order to know each other by the spirit, you must take time to _____ together.

6. With time you will learn each other's _____ and know how to _____ more effectively.

7. The LORD'S _____ PENETRATES THE HUMAN SPIRIT, EXPOSING EVERY _____ MOTIVE.

8. We need the ministry of the _____ operating in our marriage to bring us to a place of _____ the will of God and of _____ our mate.

9. The Spirit of God reveals the _____ to us and brings us to a place of _____ to God's will over our own.

HEDGE #3: TRUSTING THAT YOUR SPOUSE KNOWS THE VOICE OF GOD

"The sheep that are My own hear and are listening to My voice; and I know them, and they follow Me."[171]

1. Get to _____ how God _____ to your potential mate.

2. Get to know each other by the _____ and this will build your _____ in your mate's ability to hear from God.

3. _____ and _____ the Word each time you get together.

[171]John 10:27 AMP

4. Spend time _____ about God's Word and _____ spiritual things.

5. Your _____ for God will _____ you closer to each other.

6. It is so important to allow your spouse to _____ from God for themselves.

7. If God has _____ it, He will _____ it, and it will stand the _____ of time.

8. No one wants to be _____ by someone else.

9. If you don't _____ that your potential mate _____ the voice of God, you should not _____ them.

HEDGE #4: BEING LED BY THE SPIRIT OF GOD

"For as many as are led by the Spirit of God, they are the sons of God."[172]

1. We need to continue to _____ on the ministry of the _____ _____ as a couple.

2. When we are both _____ with God, we will be _____ with each other.

3. Begin to _____ in the _____ of the Spirit together.

4. Begin to _____ in hearing from God in _____ together.

5. God will _____ your ministry as a couple.

HEDGE #5: HONORING YOUR SPOUSE AS A CHILD OF GOD

"For he who eats and drinks in an unworthy manner

---

[172]Romans 8:14 - KJV

eatsand drinks judgment to himself, not discerning the Lord's body. For this reason many are weak and sick among you, and many sleep."[173]

1. Husbands and wives must remember that their _____ is a member of the body of Christ.

2. _____ your spouse as a child of God is rightly _____ the body of Christ.

3. The husband is called to _____ his wife like Christ _____ the church.[174]

4. The wife is called to _____ to her husband just like the church is called to _____ to Christ.[175]

5. Both are called to _____ to each other out of their _____ for God, _____ God's commandment of love.

6. The husband will not _____ of his wife being the _____ vessel.

7. The wife will not _____ _____ of her husband through _____.

8. This should be evidenced by the way they _____ their spouse in _____, as well as in _____.

9. They should not be in _____ with each other, but rather _____ their spouse over themselves.

---

[173]I Corinthians 11:29-30 - NKJV
[174]Ephesians 5:25-31 KJV
[175]Ephesians 5:22-24 KJV

CHAPTER 11 - PRACTICAL APPLICATION

BLENDING FAMILIES

"Finally, all [of you] should be of one and the same mind (united in spirit), sympathizing [with one another], loving [each other] as brethren [of one household], compassionate and courteous (tenderhearted and humble)."[176]

1. Blending families involves blending different family backgrounds, including _____ differences, _____ differences, blending _____ families, etc.. It is important to make the choice not to focus on the _____, but to be led by the spirit of God.

2. When dealing with divorced families it is important to have _____ and allow _____ for adjustments.

3. Children need _____, and are possibly dealing with feelings of _____, _____, and _____.

4. If there are feelings that your children are having a hard time talking about don't _____ them, and get _____ if you are unable to speak to your children about what they feel.

5. Many times we don't allow enough _____ for ourselves or our loved ones to _____ or deal with the emotions that divorce causes in their lives.

6. Make sure that your children know that it's not their _____ that the divorce happened and be willing to ask your children for _____ for the breakup of their family.

---

[176]I Peter 3: 8 - AMP

7. Let your children talk about how the divorce makes them feel and _____ their feelings with words of _____ and _____.

8. Whether you have lost your mate through death or divorce, time is needed to deal with the emotions of _____, _____, _____, _____, _____, _____, etc..

9. Take time to _____ these feelings and to bring them before God in _____.

10. Seek _____ _____ from other Christians who have experienced this kind of loss, and _____ _____ allowing the ministry of the Holy Spirit to bring comfort to you through His word.

11. Make sure you maintain the proper _____ in your new relationship, and don't bring your potential mate into your home overnight.

12. Remember, we are still to live a Christ like life in front of our children, even after we have made _____ in the past.

13. God's word doesn't change to fit our _____, we have to change our way of doing things to live according to God's word.

14. Sex before marriage is _____, and sex with someone other than your spouse when you are married is _____.

15. When two _____ people get married there is a lot of _____ of differences that must take place.

16. Many people think that your mate will now become a _____ of your family, or be _____ as member of your existing

family. However, you and your mate will start a _____ family that didn't previously exist, they do not just become a part of your existing family.

17. This should be seen as a new beginning with a fresh _____, and should be based on God's _____ and not the traditions or mistakes or failures of your previous family relationships.

18. Remember that your _____ should not take _____ over the word of God. If your culture teaches you to do something _____ the word of God, then you should obey God and not your culture.

19. Blending families with different _____ backgrounds should be a good experience and not something to be _____. All ethnic groups will share the same _____, and we believe God is pleased when we learn how to love all His people, regardless of their _____ differences.

20. "[In this new creation all _____ vanish.] There is no room for and there can be neither Greek nor Jew, circumcised nor uncircumcised, [nor _____ between nations whether alien] barbarians or Scythians [who are the most savage of all], nor _____ or free man; but Christ is all and in all [everything and everywhere, to _____ men, without _____ of person]."[177]

---

[177]Colossians 3:11 AMP

BLENDED FAMILY TESTIMONIAL:

For better or for worse. That is a statement in most marriage vows that represents a commitment that husbands and wives plan to keep. They make the promise that through the good times and bad, they will get through it together. However, most couples believe when they enter into their marriage that the good times will come first. When the bad times do hit, whatever they may be, they will have the memories of the good times to hold on to and give them hope that more will come. In our marriage, the worst came before the better. Most would have given up from the very beginning because our marriage looked like a hopeless marriage. We had a marriage that seemed as though it could not be restored. We didn't give up though, because of God and the dedicated couple He placed in our lives. This couple taught us how to love through the hard times.

My husband and I starting taking a premarital class with Carl and Charity Taylor a month after being engaged. We were both saved but we were not living for God at the time. The Holy Spirit was still working in us because we knew that we needed a good foundation to start our marriage. A lot of obstacles were already in front of us, so we knew we would need Godly wisdom on how to have a successful marriage. Greg, who is 15 years my senior, was recently divorced, with a daughter who at the time was 13, and I had a 1 ½ year son from a relationship out of marriage. As a part of the class, they talked about the importance of saving sexual relations for marriage. I felt led for Greg and I to stop and repent of our inappropriate relations and wait till marriage. However, when we agreed upon this, we were unaware that we were already pregnant with twins! It was a shock and overwhelming. Carl and Charity supported us and prayed for us. We finished the class and got married a short time later.

Two months after being married Carl and Charity were there for us again, at a time when we needed them most. As a 7 months pregnant newlywed I found out that my husband had relations with other women while we were dating. As a result there were two other children on the way with two different women. My world was turned upside down and my heart was broken. Thank God for Carl and Charity. They came to our house that night and about every week after for a year and a half to counsel us! With God's help, they walked us through many areas that needed healing: trust, commitment, giving, forgiving, and love.

They modeled for us that love is an action not just a feeling, or word. The time and effort they poured into our lives showed us how God's love is fully unconditional, always available, and greatly comforting. We have learned what it means to love. To love each other, all of our children, ourselves, and most importantly our God who first loved us.

Three years later, our lives are still not without trails to walk through, but we have learned where to turn when we are going through them. God is there walking us through the trails and making a way out of no way. We believe with all our hearts that God placed Carl and Charity in our lives to help save our marriage by showing unconditional love and help bring healing to all the members of our family. We are blessed to have the honor and privilege to call them our mentors and friends!

PRE-MARITAL Q & A

PRE-MARITAL Q & A

1. How often should we have date nights after marriage?

   Answer: As often as possible. It's important to maintain the bond between you, and to value the time you spend communicating and enjoying each other. This is part of cleaving.[178]

2. How much time should be spent hanging out with girl friends or guy friends?

   Answer: In the beginning of your marriage, it is important to take the time to build on your relationship. This will mean less time spent with others, including friends and family. There should be less time doing a lot of activities outside of the marriage during the first year. *"A newly married man must not be drafted into the army or be given any other official responsibilities. He must be free to spend one year at home, bringing happiness to the wife he has married."*[179] After you have built a strong foundation in your relationship, it is good to spend time with family and friends, but keep the relationship with each other as the highest priority. However, we also encourage those who have a lot of single friends to begin to develop friendships with other couples.

---

[178]Genesis 2:24 AMP
[179]Deuteronomy 24:5 NLT

3. Is recreational activity important to do regularly? Bicycling, walking, swimming, etc...?

    Answer: Recreational activities are a great way to help each other maintain a healthy lifestyle. Try to do these activities together.[180]

4. How do we come to a decision on whether to rent or buy a house?

    Answer: Follow after peace. If you both cannot agree on whether to buy a

    house, it's best to rent until you both have the peace to buy a home. Any major purchases should not be done without agreement.[181] Pray and ask God for His direction then when the time comes you will know it, because both of you will have the peace to buy with confidence. [182]

5. I have worked all my life, so when I have children I still want to work. If my husband wants me to be a stay at home mother, what steps are necessary to consider in order to make a decision?

    Answer: It is important to take the time to discuss this before marriage and if you don't agree, do not proceed with the marriage. [183] If working is important to you, he should be willing to work with you on what other arrangements can be made for your children such asChristian daycare, babysitters, or family members that will take care of the children while you both work. Remember, less time equals less influence, so

---

[180] I Timothy 4:8 KJV
[181] Amos 3:3 KJV
[182] Matthew 6:25-33 NKJV
[183] Amos 3:3 KJV

make sure you don't let others take the responsibility you have for raising your children. Be sure that they are in a safe environment with the same knowledge of God and values that you both hold.

6. Is a prenuptial agreement necessary and/or applicable for Christians?

Answer: This agreement indicates a lack of trust. It also shows a fear of losing what you have, and possibly a love for things more than a love for the potential mate. The Word of God tells us that perfect love casts out fear because fear has torment.[184] If you do not trust your potential mate, you should not marry him or her. If you marry them and they try to take what you own, remember God is your source and He will give back whatever is stolen from you.[185]

7. What is God's ideal vision of "dating" or "courtship"?

Answer: The Bible does not have an example of "dating" or "courtship," butthere are several examples of betrothal/espousal, friendships and marriage. We realize that dating or courtship means different things to different people based on their cultural background. However, most people in the U.S. think of dating as taking a friendship to a deeper level, which usually includes having sex without marriage. However, this type of relationship is not seen as God's ideal according to scripture. Several scriptures tell us that sex before marriage is fornication, which goes against God's plan for those who believe in Him.[186]

Most of the marriages mentioned in scripture were arranged

---

[184]1 John 4:18 NKJV
[185]Joel 2:23-26 KJV
[186]Ephesians 5:3; Galatians 5:19-21; I Corinthians 7:1-5 AMP

marriages, due to the culture of that day. A woman was betrothed to a man after each of their parents made the arrange-
ments. The woman and man may or may not have met prior to
their wedding day. God brought Eve to Adam and he took her to
be his wife without a courtship period. However, today due to
the change in culture and the change in family roles, there are
very few arranged marriages.

The Bible also speaks of friends being closer than a brother and
gives the example of the relationship between Jonathan and David.[187] God spoke to Moses like a friend,[188] Abraham was called
the friend of God[189] and Jesus called His disciples friends.[190]
These relationships show a closeness and a love that's based on
mutual feelings of affection and agreement; sex is not a part of
this type of relationship. The Bible also lets us know that God
designed marriage to be the relationship where sexual intimacy
is expressed without shame.

We encourage singles to form friendships with people of the
opposite sex without the pressure of traditional dating. Once
you reach the place in the friendship where you both believe you
are to marry, then the engagement period should begin. Engagement does not mean that you are now able to have sex, it means
that you are preparing for marriage. The same rules apply as
during the friendship period, only now you know that you are
ready to commit to marriage.

8. When making a list of traits of your ideal husband/wife, is it okay
    to put certain details? What would be considered too picky?

---

[187]I Samuel 18:1; 20:17 KJV
[188]Exodus 33:11 KJV
[189]James 2:23 KJV
[190]John 15:13-15 KJV

Answer: The scripture speaks of making specific requests to God,[191] and there is nothing wrong with being specific in what you want in a mate. God was very detailed in His design of the tabernacle down to the hooks and latches, so we can't overwhelm Him with the details. However, remember your best match is the one God leads you to, and perfection is defined by the spirit of the man or woman. Getting to know the person by the spirit first will help you know whether they are the right person for you.[192]

9. What would be considered "preparation" when waiting for your husband/wife?

Answer: Preparation starts with your relationship with God. This includes making sure that you know and understand the unconditional love of God, and that you have experienced God's love and are ready to love someone in that same way. Take the time to examine yourself and be sure that you are whole and not dealing with the results of brokenness or wounding. Take a class and read books on marriage and family relationships; preferably those written from a Christian perspective. Prepare financially with education and employment. Be led by the Spirit of God, praying in the spirit, building yourself up in faith.[193]

10. Do you answer the phone while in the middle of a personal conversation?

Answer: No, it is important to make your relationship with each other a higher priority than all others. If the call was important, the caller will leave a message or call back. When you finish the conversation you can always return the call.

[191]Philippians 4:6 AMP
[192]Romans 8:5 AMP
[193]Jude 1:20-21 AMP

11. How much love, kisses, hugs, or affectionate touching, should we show in front of our kids?

    Answer: We believe it is important for children to see a healthy display of affection between their parents. However, save the passion for your private time, behind closed doors. A hug, gentle kiss, or even holding hands or cuddling is okay to display in front of your kids.

12. If I have a problem with his/her parents or if I don't always get along with them, what should I do?

    Answer: It is important to make sure both of your parents are in agreement with your relationship before you get married. You want their blessing. However, as we mentioned in chapter 4, find out what is behind the disagreement. After the marriage, you are expected to walk in unity, and your parents cannot take priority over your spouse.

13. What is the best way to tell our parents to back out of our lives, but not fully stay out?

    Answer: We want to say again that it is important to get your parents blessing before you marry. Even if you don't have spiritual parents, they normally want the best for you, so don't shut them out. You may be an adult, but you can still benefit from your parent's wisdom. If you do not have a good relationship with your parents, or if their advice goes against the Word of God, you must respectfully hear them out but you do not have to agree to do anything that goes against God's Word. Remember to follow after peace and walk in the love of God.

14. If one spouse's parents agree to the union, and the other spouse's parents don't, should they get married?

Answer: Find out why the other spouse's parents don't agree to the marriage. You need the blessing of both parents, if possible. It is important to fully examine the reasons why the other spouse's parents don't agree. Don't proceed with the marriage until all questions have been answered. Make sure you are not walking in the flesh but are being led by the Spirit. Seek counsel from a pastor, a spiritual leader in the church or another strong spiritual couple.

15. Does having sex or having a child outside of marriage obligate two people to get married?

Answer: No. As we have said before, the Word of God calls sex outside of marriage, fornication or sin. This does not obligate you to marry the person you sinned with, nor does having a child as a result of this relationship. It is important to be led by the Spirit and not by the flesh, especially when deciding whom to marry.

16. How can we know how to communicate when we are afraid of conflict?

Answer: Choose to walk in unconditional love, especially when you have a conflict or a difference of opinion. The word of God says; *"There is no fear in **love**; but **perfect love casts** out fear, because fear involves torment. But he who fears has not been made **perfect** in **love**."*[194] The fear that is involved in conflict has to do with being rejected or not feeling accepted due to a difference. It is important to realize that just because you have a difference of opinion does not mean you don't still love the person. Over time you will learn each other's ways and know how to handle differences without conflict, as long as you choose to walk in

---

[194] 1 John 4:18 NKJV, emphasis mine

love. Allow the fruit of the Spirit to operate in the midst of a disagreement and have self control.[195] Speak in the right spirit, don't attack each other. Remember that words are seeds, so sow the words you want to receive back.

17. How do we deal with our different levels of faith and belief?

Answer: As we have mentioned before, it is important not to be unequally yoked with an unbeliever[196], and this also relates to the difference of faith and belief. For example, if you believe in tithing, but your future mate is unwilling to tithe, this is un-equally yoked. However, there is still room for growth, if your mate does not tithe, but is willing to learn and agrees to do it by faith. If you don't agree on how big of an offering to give, be willing to start on the level of faith that both of you can agree on and grow in your faith together. It is also important to state that if you are of two different beliefs, for example you are a Christian and they're religion doesn't believe that Jesus is the Son of God, there is no agreement without compromising what the word of God says. The bible clearly tells us that we should not consider being married to or unequally yoked with an unbeliever.

18. Is it important to be open about our finances and share our fi-nances?

Answer: There should be no secrets about financial debts, secret bank accounts or secret stashes of money. If you cannot trust your potential mate you shouldn't marry them. However, af-ter you are married you should be completely open and honest about money and share the same bank account. You will learn a lot about each other's spending habits and it will take time to

---

[195]Galatians 5:22-25 NKJV
[196]II Corinthians 6:14 KJV

adjust to sharing your finances. However, you must be willing to trust each other. This can be very difficult for someone who has been independent for a long time and is use to making all the financial decisions for themselves. However, the two are meant to become one, and this is an area that will cause you to grow in trust and in you love for each other. Be willing to take a financial class together and come into agreement concerning money. Love God and each other more than you love money.[197]

19. How open should I be about previous relationships and life experiences?

Answer: You should be willing to be transparent with your mate about previous relationships, but that doesn't mean that you need to give every detail. Be willing to answer questions honestly about your experiences. Find out your mate's testimony and share your own. Before you marry, you should be at the fifth level of communication with your mate. This means you are totally open and honest with each other without fear.

20. What if we don't agree on furniture for the house?

Answer: Don't let selfishness rob you of the intimacy in your relationship. Be willing to compromise on the small stuff. Having furniture is important, but it is not as important as being able to enjoy the home you share with each other. By love, serve one another.[198]

21. Does not caring about how the house is decorated mean I have a non-caring attitude?

Answer: Remember, you are marrying someone who is different

---

[197]Matthew 6:24 AMP
[198]Galatians 5:13 KJV

than you. It is okay if one of you loves to decorate, and the other one doesn't. Just be willing to listen and show some interest.

22. What should we do if one of our relatives wants to move in with us?

Answer: It is important that you have time to cleave to one another, and having someone move in with you will take time away from cleaving. In the first year of your marriage, you need to be able to establish the foundation of your relationship with each other. This will mean spending time alone together as often as you can. Having a relative, especially a parent, in your home will get in the way of cleaving. Your parents and your relatives still see you as an individual and will treat you as separate individuals. They will parent you and stop the development of oneness in your relationship with your spouse.[199]

23. If your spouse is a morning person and they read their Bible in the morning, should you adjust your reading schedule to fit theirs?

Answer: It doesn't matter if you read the Bible in the morning together, but it is important that you take time to read the Bible together during the day. Keep your time of personal devotion between you and the Lord, but make it a priority to spend time together in prayer and reading of the Word each day. There is power in agreement.[200]

24. Should you both go to bed at the same time?

Answer: Yes. Make it a practice to go to bed together as this will help you cleave to one another. If you are unable to due to work

---

[199]Genesis 2:24-25 KJV
[200]Ecclesiastes 4:12 AMP

or some unexpected delay, or children, be willing to make ad
justments, but don't let this become a normal practice.

25. Is it okay to change your location during an "argument" or to
spend some time alone?

Answer: Remember to take the word "argument" out of your
vocabulary. You will have disagreements, but arguments spring
forth strife and every evil work.[201] Disagreements just need one
word from God to bring an answer or resolution. Pray first, before you trying to resolve any disagreement. It is okay to wait
until you can speak in the right spirit, but don't separate unless
it is for a short time and then come back together to talk. If you
need time to pray and think before you speak, tell your spouse
you need some time to pray and think, but agree on a time to
come together and talk.[202]Don't give your spouse the silent treatment.[203]

26. Should we pray before sex and after?

Answer: Yes. Jesus is in you and He should be acknowledged at
all times.[204] If you bring Him into the marriage bed with you,
He will help make it a fulfilling experience for both of you. He
will help keep the sexual intimacy between you and your spouse
pure. It will be a joyous experience without shame.[205]

27. How often should we have sex?

Answer: "Do not refuse and deprive and defraud each other [of
your due marital rights], except perhaps by mutual consent for a*

---

[201]James 3:16 KJV
[202]Ephesians 4:26-27 AMP
[203]I Corinthians 13:11 AMP
[204]Proverbs 3:5-6 KJV
[205]Genesis 2:24-25 KJV

time, so that you may devote yourselves unhindered to prayer. But afterwards resume marital relations, lest Satan tempt you [to sin] through your lack of restraint of sexual desire."[206] It is important to be open with your spouse about your need for sexual fulfillment. Come together often in the beginning of your relationship. Remember that sex is not just physical: it is an expression of emotion and affection, it is intellectual, it builds intimacy, it is a time when spiritual oneness occurs, and it is part of the cleaving process.

[206]I Corinthians 7:5 AMP

APPLICATION FOR MARRIAGE

PURPOSE OF THIS APPLICATION

The purpose of this application is to target areas that need healing or sharpening before marriage. It is our desire that you be prepared to enter into the covenant of marriage; remember, *"And though a man might prevail against him who is alone, two will withstand him. A three-fold cord is not quickly broken."*[207] You can be assured that as you walk in agreement with your spouse and put Jesus first, you will have the added power of agreement spoken of in this scripture.

It is important to take this time to root out any blind spots or holes that may result in major problems in your marriage.

We also hope that this application will be a tool to be used by marriage counselors, clergy and those in church leadership who are involved in pre-marital preparation. Our desire is to arm the people of God with spiritual weapons to protect their marriage and to ultimately to eliminate divorce out of the Body of Christ.

Always remember, *"So then faith cometh by hearing, and hearing by the word of God."*[208]

God Bless You!

Carl & Charity Taylor

---

[207]Ecclesiastes 4:12 AMP
[208]Romans 10:17 KJV

MARRIAGE APPLICATION

Last Name		First		M.I.	Date

Street Address	Apartment/Unit #

City	State	ZIP

Phone	E-mail Address

Date Available	Social Security No.	Desired Salary

Position Applied for

Are you a citizen of the United States?   YES ☐   NO ☐   If no, are you authorized to work in the U.S.?   YES ☐   NO ☐

Have you ever been convicted of a felony?   YES ☐   NO ☐   If yes, explain

EDUCATION

High School			Address		
From	To	Did you graduate?	YES ☐ NO ☐	Degree	
College			Address		
From	To	Did you graduate?	YES ☐ NO ☐	Degree	
Other			Address		
From	To	Did you graduate?	YES ☐ NO ☐	Degree	

REFERENCES

Please list three references; include at least one professional reference.

Full Name	Relationship
Company	Phone ( )
Address	

Full Name	Relationship
Company	Phone ( )
Address	

Full Name	Relationship
Company	Phone ( )
Address	

EMPLOYMENT HISTORY

Company	Phone ( )
Address	Supervisor

Job Title	Starting Salary $	Ending Salary $

Responsibilities

From	To	Reason for Leaving

May we contact your previous supervisor for a reference?   YES ☐   NO ☐

Company	Phone ( )
Address	Supervisor .

Job Title	Starting Salary $	Ending Salary $

Responsibilities

From	To	Reason for Leaving

May we contact your previous supervisor for a reference?   YES ☐   NO ☐

Company	Phone ( )
Address	Supervisor

Job Title	Starting Salary $	Ending Salary $

Responsibilities

From	To	Reason for Leaving

May we contact your previous supervisor for a reference?   YES ☐   NO ☐

MILITARY SERVICE

Branch	From To
Rank at Discharge	Type of Discharge

If other than honorable, explain

PERSONAL & FINANCIAL BACKGROUND

Have you ever been married before?   YES ☐   NO ☐

From	To	If divorced, explain

Have you had any premarital counseling?   YES ☐   NO ☐   How many hours?

Counselor's Name	Title
Name of Program/Class	Phone ( )

PERSONALITY TRAITS

Circle the personality traits that best describe your personality. Total the circled items and then times the total by 2. Put your total score on the line listed in each box. Chart your score on the line graph with a dot and then connect the dots with a line.

Personality Type A		Personality Type B	
Aggressive	Determined	Risk	Energetic
Bold	Firm	Motivator	Creative
Purpose Driven	Goal Oriented	Fun Lover	Enjoys Variety
Competitive	Leader	Verbal	Likes Change
Enterprising	Decisive	Optimistic	Animated
Self Motivated	Adventurous	Avoids	Spontaneous
Enjoys Challenges	Independent	Social	Practical Joker
"Get it done."		"Everything's going to be alright."	
Total X 2 = ____		Total X 2 = ____	

Personality Type C		Personality Type D	
Thoughtful	Adaptable		Musical
Nurturing	Avoids Conflict	Practical	Deep
Peace Maker	Even Tempered	Detailed	Orderly
Enjoys Routine	Patient	Persistent	Predictable
Sympathetic	Shy	Skeptical	Analytical
Friendly	Tolerant	Factual	Discerning
Loyal	Good Listener	Cultured	Scheduled
"I won't hurt you."		"Do it right the first time."	

PERSONALITY CHART

	Type A	Type B	Type C	Type D
28	—	—	—	—
	—	—	—	—
	—	—	—	—
	—	—	—	—
	—	—	—	—
	—	—	—	—
	—	—	—	—
20	—	—	—	—
	—	—	—	—
	—	—	—	—
	—	—	—	—
	—	—	—	—
	—	—	—	—
	—	—	—	—
	—	—	—	—
	—	—	—	—
10	—	—	—	—
	—	—	—	—
	—	—	—	—
	—	—	—	—
	—	—	—	—
	—	—	—	—
	—	—	—	—
0				

Now that you have your score, turn to the next page to see what additional strengths and weaknesses your personality may have. Remember, not to feel limited by your personality but to continue to grow and mature. Don't make excuses for an area of weakness.

"And His gifts were [varied; He Himself appointed and gave men to us] some to be apostles (special messengers), some prophets (inspired preachers and expounders), some evangelists (preachers of the Gospel, traveling missionaries), some pastors (shepherds of His flock) and teachers. His intention was the perfecting and the full equipping of the saints (His consecrated people), [that they should do] the work of ministering toward building up Christ's body (the church), [That it might develop] until we all attain oneness in the faith and in the comprehension of the [full and accurate] knowledge of the Son of God, that [we might arrive] at really mature manhood (the completeness of personality which is nothing less than the standard height of Christ's own perfection), the measure of the stature of the fullness of the Christ and the completeness found in Him."
Ephesians 4:11-13 AMP

Personality Type A		Personality Type B	
Strengths	**Weaknesses**	**Strengths**	**Weaknesses**
Persuasive	Impatient	Refreshing	Undisciplined
Productive	Proud	Funny	Impulsive
Self-reliant	Domineering	Playful	Procrastinator
Confident	Bossy	Lively	Disorganized
Practical	Unaffectionate	Popular	Inconsistent
Outspoken	Short-tempered	Convincing	Loud
Leader	Workaholic	Inspiring	Show-off

This personality must learn to:

    a) Value people more than projects.
    b) Take time for relaxation.
    c) Express their anger constructively.

This personality must learn to:

    a) Follow things through to the finish.
    b) Deal with the tough issues of life.
    c) Be more committed.

Personality Type C		Personality Type D	
Strengths	**Weaknesses**	**Strengths**	**Weaknesses**
Balanced	Worrier	Inquisitive	Revengeful
Contented	Sluggish	Artistic	Withdrawn
Inoffensive	Compromising	Honest	Pessimistic
Neat	Unenthusiastic	Respectful	Insecure
Satisfied	Uninvolved	Consistent	Unforgiving
Submissive	Aimless	Loyal	Introverted
Reserved	Indecisive	Precise	Critical

This personality must learn:

    a) You can't solve everyone's problems.
    b) You must trust God and release people to Him.
    c) Not to become a man pleaser.
    d) To say no.

This personality must learn:

    a) Nothing is as bad as it seems or as good as it sounds.
    b) Don't be extreme and allow yourself to become depressed.
    c) Trust God.

DISCLAIMER & SIGNATURE

I certify that my answers are true and complete to the best of my knowledge.

I understand that false or misleading information in my application may result in an unhealthy marital relationship. I understand that I may also be denied the use of the church/marital facilities at _____, and/or additional counseling may be required before marriage.

Signature

Date

Prayer Of Salvation

Now that you have read the book, if you have not already received Jesus Christ as your Savior and Lord, we want you to know these four important things:

1. **Who Jesus is.**

   He was born of God, according to Matthew 1:18, *"Now the birth of Jesus Christ was as follows: After His mother Mary was betrothed to Joseph, before they came together, she was found with child of the Holy Spirit."*[209] Verses 22,23 say *"Now all this was done, that it might be fulfilled which was spoken of the Lord by the prophet, saying, Behold, a virgin shall be with child, and shall bring forth a son, and they shall call his name EMMANUEL, which being interpreted is, GOD WITH US."*[210]

   He is the Son of God and the Saviour of the world, according to John 3:16, 17, *"For GOD so loved the world, that HE GAVE HIS ONLY BEGOTTEN SON, that whosoever believeth on him should not perish, but have everlasting life. For God sent not HIS SON into the world to condemn the world; but THAT THE WORLD THROUGH HIM MIGHT BE SAVED."*[211]

2. **What Jesus came to do.**

   In Luke 4:18, Jesus said of himself, *"The Spirit of the LORD IS UPON ME, BECAUSE HE HAS ANOINTED ME TO PREACH THE GOSPEL TO THE POOR; HE HAS SENT ME TO HEAL THE BROKENHEARTED, TO PROCLAIM LIBERTY TO THE CAPTIVES AND RECOVERY OF SIGHT TO THE BLIND, to*

---

[209]emphasis mine
[210]emphasis mine
[211]emphasis mine

set at liberty those who are oppressed"[212] That means he came to set you and me free!

He came to die for our sins. John 15:13 says, *"Greater love has no one than this, than to LAY DOWN HIS LIFE FOR HIS FRENDS."*[213] I Timothy 1:15 says, *"...Christ Jesus came into the world to SAVE SINNERS;..."*[214] And Romans 5:8 says, *"But God demonstrates His own love toward us, in that while we were still sinners, CHRIST DIED FOR US."*[215]

3. Why we need Jesus.

Romans 3:23, tells us why, *"For all have sinned, and come short of the glory of God;"* Even those who are morally good need Jesus.[216] Isaiah 64:6 says, *"..., and all our righteousness is as filthy rags;..."*[217] And finally, Romans 6:23 says, *"For the wages of sin is death; BUT THE GIFT OF GOD IS ETERNAL LIFE THROUGH JESUS CHRIST OUR LORD."*[218]

4. How to receive Jesus as Saviour.

Now that you know all that Jesus is and what He has done out of His love for you, all that's left is to receive Him. If this is your desire, repeat this simple prayer:

Dear Father, in the name of Jesus. I acknowledge that I am a sinner in need of a Savior. I confess Jesus as my Lord and Savior according to Your Word.

Father, I believe that Jesus died and rose again so that I could

[212]emphasis mine
[213]emphasis mine
[214]emphasis mine
[215]emphasis mine
[216]emphasis mine
[217]emphasis mine
[218]emphasis mine

have eternal life. I ask for forgiveness for my sin of unbelief, and right now I confess Jesus as my Saviour and Lord. From this day forward, I put my life in Your hands. In Jesus' name, Amen!

If you meant that prayer, you are saved according to Romans 10:9, which says, *"That if you confess with your mouth the Lord Jesus and believe in your heart that God has raised Him from the dead, you will be saved."*[219]

---

[219]emphasis mine

WELCOME TO THE FAMILY OF GOD!

Write to us at Higher Life Ministries, c/o Carl & Charity Taylor, 1216 E. Kenosha St, PMB#106, Broken Arrow, OK 74012. We'd like to hear from you.

RECOMMENDED READING

Before You Say I Do; *by H. Norman Wright, Wes Roberts. (1997). Eugene, OR, United States: Harvest House Publishers*

His Needs Her Needs; *by Willard F. Harley Jr. Fifteenth Anniversary Edition (2001). Grand Rapids, MI, United States: Published by Fleming H. Revell a division of Baker Book House Company, 2001.*

Love Busters; *by Willard F. Harley Jr. (2002). Grand Rapids, MI, United States: Published by Fleming H. Revell a division of Baker Book House Company, 2002.*

The Five Love Languages; *by Gary Chapman. (1992). United States: Moody Publishers*

If Only He Knew: Understanding Your Wife; *by Gary Smalley. Zondervan Publishing House, 1982.*

For Better or For Best: Understanding Your Husband; *by Gary Smalley. (1982). United States: Zondervan Publishing House, 1982.*

ABOUT THE AUTHORS

Carl received Jesus Christ as savior at the age of 14, and Charity received salvation at the age of 11. They both received the baptism in the Holy Spirit in their teens.

The Lord laid on Carl's heart to attend Bible School at the age of 16, at Deliverance Bible Institute, Newark, NJ. He started preaching at 16, and began teaching Sunday School and Bible School at the age of 18. When Carl was 20 years old the Lord laid on his heart to attend Rhema Bible Training Center by Correspondence.

Carl and Charity were married on May 4, 1985, at the age of 20 and 22 and soon afterward became Assistant Pastors at Lighthouse Tabernacle Ministry, Staten Island, NY, under the late Bishop Harry S. Thompson, Charity's dad. They started a radio ministry called Faith Deliverance Ministry that aired for three and a half years.

In 1997 the Lord led them to Tulsa, OK, and then to Victory Christian Center. Carl attended Victory Bible Institute in 1999. They began teaching cell groups in 2000, and began to teach a Sunday School connect group called, "Before You Say I Do", about six years ago, which meets every Sunday morning at 9:30 am. They are also members of Victory Fellowship of Ministries. Carl and Charity have been guests on Christian TV programs in their local area.

They have three children, Joel, Evonne and Carl Jr., and three grandchildren, Gabrielle, Makayla and Elijah.

The Harrison House Vision

Proclaiming the truth and the power

Of the Gospel of Jesus Christ

With excellence;

Challenging Christians to

Live victoriously,

Grow spiritually,

Know God intimately.